A box full of hair.

135 East Park can still rat... ... .
recall visiting the edifice.
It was just past Park and Main and my day to week journeys passed here and the Pit's precipice.
I approached the building with high caution unsure of what lay in wait behind the dirty glass.
I would garner my strength and take a deep breath, entering before my courage would pass.

I never made it more than four or five kid size steps inside when I would have to pause in awe.
There we faceless filthy mannequins askew and undressed hanging from the ceilings and walls.
I then would start wandering the creaking well-traveled wood floor, byways through nothing.
A Zen store as it had everything and nothing for that special person who is not non-existing.

The expeditions were far and few in between so each time an odd or scary as hell piece was found.
The day I found a box of hair made me second guess the inventory and how long it'd been around.
I never did make a purchase there as my Mom would have me and the purchase on the back porch.
I have no idea if the proprietor made any money on goods, which for public service should see a torch.

You got to give the Son of Bitch credit where credit is due for he made his mark on the Mining City.
He was a perennial entry in the Fourth of July parade and was Grand Marshall for a Saint Paddy's.
I still to this day have more than a question or two about one of Buttes most off colored individuals.
Let's start with his appearance as it became his trade mark, pushing the limits on business casual.

I never knew where he got the kids to walk with him in the parade, as I recall that he never had a kid.
I felt for that costumed troop that got drafted on the Fourth, likely punishment for something they did.
I never got physically close to the gentleman so of his hygiene and grooming I observed from afar.
I gathered he rolled around in a pile of clothes each morning and left his false teeth in the hall jar.

I don't recall a big deal outside an announcement in The Standard of when he passed away.
I can only imagine the Herculean task that was involved in cleaning out his estate every day.
It had to take a month of Sundays and I can only imagine the oddities found preserved in salt.
I think they should have made the effort and got Geraldo Rivera, to open Tony the Trader's vault.

The Sixth Floor.

I have visited more than a few garages and out buildings throughout the Mining Camp.
It was a variety of reasons from tasting fire in a bottle of grapo to borrowing a camping lamp.
These are the original man caves I speak of, long before the phrase became a cliché name'.
They had wood shops and tools instead of video games but welcoming all just the same.

Home brews were made, vino was bottled and some of the best elk sausage was ground.
At the larger operations it was like walking into Ace hardware where anything could be found.
Many had every tool one would need to build a house and every type of specialized tools.
In honesty many of the tools and materials were collected by breaking the Sixth Floor's rules.

There were shovels and picks thrown in the back of a truck or a hammer in a lunch bucket.
There were nails and electrical wiring for the new addition and the vehicle that trucked it.
It is no secret that tons of material somehow grew legs and walked away from the mines.
A cement mixer to pour a floor for the new bedroom pulled week end duty a few times.

Lumber was consumed by the Company and more than a few boards went through the side gate.
Every item approved on the Sixth Floor of the Company to mine copper could easily dissipate.
Not everyone pilfered yet when the company was rolling the spending to mine was large.
I heard stories of large home projects and remodeled additions some as big as a barge.

I am sure there are many urban stories on how the Company helped an employee build,
Yet I never heard of anybody getting arrested, it was a silent and stealth building guild.
All the tools that made it off the mine yard site found a home where they did stay.
I can only imagine if those free shopping trips were around today with an account on Ebay.

I saw collections of tools that found their way past the Burnsie's and stored in some ones barn.
It was never discussed or brought up in the bar as it was serious business not a social yarn.
No one looked at it as stealing because it came from the company not down the street.
In the end the company got even and destroyed everything they helped build, only not as discreet.

An empty glass reflects light.

I have never been much on Martini bars if I ended up there it was by pure accident.
I like working man bars and the female bartenders who work there to cover the rent.
These are the bars where the drinks are stiff yet priced with a patron's wallet in mind.
A fight can break out over a bad keno game or reacting to the TV's umpire that's blind.

The best of this genre of saloon can be found in even the smaller of Montana towns.
The Oxford, the M and M and the Lobby are a few where I have put whiskey shots down.
In Kalispell behind the Oxford Bar on Main was one of the best saloons of them all.
A tough little joint where you had to watch your back, known as "The Hole in the Wall"

In these roust about days and nights rambling like loose cattle in the saloons of the Big Sky.
I drank and battled with Indians off the reservation some thinking it a wish to die.
Nothing could be further from the truth as no one walking the earth enjoyed a drink as me.
I was living large, I was chasing the clouds looking back I recognize my dumb ass stupidity.

I walked away and by my aches and pains I am reminded to admit that I am very much alive.
I take the time even today to remember those had drinking lads and lassies that didn't survive.
There was Tim the sheet rocking prison cowboy who died in below freezing temps under the bridge.
Trish the Dish, hard drinking beauty her blind grandmother's eyes left on a Green River ledge.

I remember their ending for the simple reason because I was there in the middle and their beginning.
Like me they enjoyed two for one happy hours held at noon in the middle of week instead of working.
I looked down the tracks and saw that journey was running out of rails so I chose to disembark.
I guess they were enjoying the drink and dining car and forgot to get off before it turned dark.

There is no taking back those times bending back the arms of the clock until it forgives.
I work in my garden and stare a blank paper wondering how I dodged life's prison shivs.
I have a suitcase of stories, a liver that still talks to me and I realize just how good it can be.
I won't be on my death bed counting missed chances I am living outside my history.

The Sawbuck that never left the bar.

During the summer of 76 I had come back to Butte to relax and enjoy the Montana weather.
I would be heading back out in September for a radio gig making the vacation even better.
It was a tight group of guys that I ran with those months filling our time with golf and tennis.
Wagers were lost and won by all in those summer months for which Montana is famous.

There was no bar in particular that would offer respite to take a break from the hot day,
Maloney's and McQueen shared entertainment duties with McGrath at the old Speedway.
I was a well paid artist for the State of Montana drawing a weekly unemployment check.
It was the same predicament for many of the others so money never demanded respect.

One afternoon at Maloney's I found one of my buddies was running short on his cash.
Being a pal I loaned him a twenty, which had been doodled on with ink, out of my stash.
The twenty went back to the bar till as he ordered a beverage and bought me a drink.
I saw the twenty come back out of the till for another pals change and I started to think.

The next day we returned to Maloney's for a drink and the twenty showed up again.
It had somehow dodged the last bank deposit and here he story gets very interesting.
The twenty went back in the till and found its way in and out of the busy bars till.
It would come out and given when a big bill was broken for a patron to get his fill.

The twenty made its way to the bathroom where it was used for an illegal transaction.
It came out of the bathroom ending up on the bar and soon was back in the action.
This doodled on bill remained in the bar for more than a week going through many hands.
It started to get very odd as it continually appeared in many of the bars transactions.

The novelty wore off after a couple of weeks but that twenty stuck around for a while.
In and out of our pockets and wallets being spent and then loaned we started to smile.
That twenty dollar bill stood for our friendship as it was handled among the crew.
The sawbuck saw more traffic and continued to be traded for a couple drinks or two.

The novelty of the curious currency kept coming up again in a conversation with my brother.
To know it was borrowed and traded as it made the rounds made is special from all other.
I think of this twenty that changed many hands as it held its place in our friendly, easy lives.
One thing I know it would never happened if we were not single and had to explain to wives.

The bill reminded us all how lucky we were in our times and how close we all truly were,
That bill touched so many of my friends lives that summer, I think back and saw it occur.
We were all the best of friends and willing to give to each other or debate any kind of help.
Had a woman been involved watching the purse strings we would be beaten until we yelp.

Saint Paddy.

And yet another St. Paddy's day has met me with the sunrise
It is the seventh or eighth I've been sober if I am correct to surmise.
It is a sober feast day for this Paddy of the South East.
I'll give the world a break from me being a drunken beast.

The morning is welcome with coffee, cream and sugar,
Not a couple of fingers of Whiskey or a cup of the cure.
I will not be reviving my glorious thirst,
That torch has been tampered for better not worse.

No fights in in the alley's or tables to dance on,
No swinging my shillelagh or pulling my pants down,
Telling the world to puga ma hone and being the clown.
No wondering the haunted Pubs of Butte my home town.

But I wish nothing but the best for those who partake,
Celebrating the saint who freed Ireland from the snakes.
Be kind to each other and toast those who are not here.
Be not sad for us missing, be of nothing but good cheer

I used to drink Guinness, For Bubba Maloney it was Bud Light
Just find a safe passage at the end the night.
So raise a glass and toast me, and for God's sake sing a song
For the party is today, and of this earth we are not long.

The Kennedy's and Butte.

I walked into the back door of the house assured I was about to startle my Mom,
The startling had been done before I arrived; Walter Cronkite had dropped the bomb.
The General Electric portable TV was informing the small crowd gathered in the kitchen
 Catholics nationwide had been force to their knees to pray, their cores had been shaken.

We know the story; there is no need to rehash it, no need to visit that dark stain.
What is worth noting and deserves a look is how visiting Butte was a political gain.
From Harding to the Kennedy's and most recently Obama and his message for change.
Butte is the place for the power brokers to visit bypassing all other cities on the range.

Lindbergh, Nixon and Harry Truman all spent the night at the Grand old Finlen,
Jack and Jackie stayed before he became President but it is Bobby's visit why this written.
Growing up we all held a muck a muck above it all, if you will above the fray.
I thought Dick Butkis walked on water, for Sunday games I prayed the Bears would play.

At the bottom of our stair way the first thing you saw was a picture of the Pope.
On the western wall in an average frame was JFK, the great Irish man of Hope.
We prayed for the President in our morning school prayers led by the teaching Nun.
We were indoctrinated with the wit and wiles of the movie star like favorite Irish son.

When Jack went down and as far as that moment I cared only about getting the school day off.
By that afternoon my household mood has darkened and I realized I could no longer scoff.
Even at that early age I felt the edge of destiny had shifted the ever so slightest degree.
I was reassured by the adults after Jack was buried that the torch had been passed onto Bobby.

The years did pass and the predictions came true when Bobby stepped up to the plate.
He hit the trail to bring about the change we needed and with Butte he set a date.
He arrived in town and worked the crowd as he travelled to Naranche Stadium.
And like trout eating pellets in fishery, we school children swarmed when he did come.

His car pulled over at Front and Delaware and he waded into the waist high crowd.
He shook my hand like he did a thousand others but for some reason I was on a cloud.
He looked at me and the others and every one of us thought he was talking to just one.
I was quite sure this was how the all the Apostles felt after the last supper was done.

He rolled back to his car and continued over Front Street to be seen again on the campaign.
Like the rest of the nation we followed it up to LA and Bobby was never heard from again.
I will never forget what happened to me on that street corner the day I shook Bobby's hand.
I would have given that day from school off back to the Nuns if they could have served this land.

Ape in the Chinese Laundry.

I am rightfully proud and mention often my Dad Jack McGinley's service as a Butte Fireman.
The Butte Archives has his helmet on display in the Hose Tower a great honor for this Irishman.
Jack had over twenty five years on his time clock before he rolled out on his last fire call.
I am blessed with the memories of my visits to the old Fire House, I was six and in total awe.

As one would imagine like any other Butte Institution there were many a good story to tell.
So many close calls and fighting fires in 30 below temps brought caution with every fire bell.
I once saw a picture of my Dad fighting a fire, and the water is freezing and the land is ice.
A fellow fire fighter is breaking the ice off his helmet front, a sheet that is covering his eyes.

Fire Fighters have always had my deepest respect as I believe they give more than other jobs.
Every Fighter will tell you they love what they're doing; leaving hob nobbing to the Hob Nobs.
As with any job that carries a high risk and danger it seems they have the best stories to tell.
Scars are better than tattoo's because the stories are better, especially when you got them in hell.

There was the story of the Butte Fighter, I think his name was Casagranda, he fell off a moving fire truck.
He was hanging on back and let go to bless him self as he passed Saint Joe's Church, just pure bad luck.
There were mishaps and more than a few times Dad had some great stories for us boys about his shift.
The story that stands out more than any other involves China town and a large monkey that was miffed.

The Cat Houses were still open and gambling is big, the Mining Camps citizens are bending the law.
China Town was active and the laboring jewel of the Treasure State is growing, bustling and raw.
At the turn of the century Butte had close to a thousand Oriental's living within a few city blocks.
Historical artifacts show that opium dens were once active underground, really not much of a shock.

One night a fire call was issued for a building in China Town with access through the back alley.
The uptown station made the quick downhill run with all trucks and abled men on site to rally.
The fire was in the basement area of the wood structure, a labyrinth not visited by most whites.
China town was a secret and very exotic world ruled by the occupants who had no civil rights.

The fire was knocked down and my Dad and Marty Hanley were sent in to give it a look.
They were looking for hot spots while being the first explorers in the hallways and nooks.
They were using headlamps as the electricity was lost; it was as black as the inside of a cow.
This is when the primate decided to grace the men with an appearance and a dark, deep bellow.

Marines testify there is nothing more intense than the engaging in a closed quarter battle.
My Dad said his startled yell along with Marty's and the Monkey's was more than a chortle.
All three decided to go the same way at the same time and in the scuffle Marty got hurt.
They made it outside and took Marty to the Hospital and my Dad told the story in blurts.

Marty ended up get a series of painful shots for tetanus and rabies just to be the safe side.
The King Kong of the laundry disappeared so the police went in to find out where he could hide.
There was a quick rally of shots about five minutes later the monkey got carried out on board.
The lesson was that you never know what will occur at a fire, or what a Chinaman may hoard.

Bill Thomas/Party Line/Breakfast at the Nite Owl Bar.

I was working for Shag Miller at KBOW I was doing the overnight shift and covering for Bill Thomas on Party Line in the afternoon.
Shag was young and very enterprising he was the guy who brought Muzak into elevators and he was whistling a profitable tune.
It was one of my first radio gigs full time, Steve Sevenor was doing the mornings and for about a year I was the first thing Sevenor saw as I did the overnights live.
Sevenor wore rainbow suspenders, had two poodles that looked like him, he loved a good jug of vino and liked to say "All that Jive".

Now I am all of 19, so I am getting paid to do what I love, though I knew I was no Fred Kenny to spend my career at one station.
This is not the bottom of the broadcast rung it actually it was where radio is important but I decided early to travel the nation
I learned to call games, sell carpet at live remotes but the best part was to cover for Bill Thomas who was at the near end of his radio career.
What I remember about Bill he had the patience of a vulture dealing with the Butte callers which is probably why he liked his beer.

I was out selling High School sport packages and stopped by the world famous Nite Owl Bar to get them on with some ad's for the game.
At ten o'clock sitting at the bar is my uncle Pat Thompson getting well with Bill as they drank a Butte breakfast with no shame.

I talked with fellas for a few minutes passing on the offer for a drink.
Little did I now I would be holding Bill's tie later as he was bent over a bathroom sink.
I said my good byes and headed out the door to make a few more sales calls. Within a few hours I would be hosting party line doing my best not to stink.

I need to clarify now I had nothing but respect for Bill Thomas and what became fifty plus years call in radio show.
But being Butte that it is, when our vices were ignored and more than one time a person would go to work with a glow.
So that fine day I stopped back at the studio and Shag pulled me aside, Bill was not doing well he had to go home.
I would take the air that after noon, my first talk show appearance Shag advised me to hold the reigns and not let callers roam.

I remember not one caller or what I might have said and I assure you I remember not one topic the citizens of Butte harped and goad.
But somehow I got through it, all the commercials got played and Shag quietly acknowledged I could do the show later on down the road.
As far as Bill goes he made it back from the edge and for many years he continued to host the first of its kind on Shags radio station.
It started my long radio career, I did many talk shows and Shag and Bill I tagged along in my spirit as I did radio throughout the nation.

Saint Paddy's Day 2013

When Columbus Day comes about I don't dress up like Galileo.
I don't drink wine, make peperoni Pizza and yell out Mama Mia.
Native Americans have Pow Wows and dress in skins and feathers
I don't put on war paint nor do I wear Elk skin turned into leather.

The Gays have their pride parades, their costumes are resplendent,
I don't partake, I'm not gay, and it's their day to be totally decadent.
The Scottish have no holidays of which I am aware.
And if they did, I would wear no kilt, I probably would not care.

African Americans celebrate a great man on Martin Luther King Day.
It is now a national holiday and with that I am quite OK.
The Hispanics have Cinco de Mayo which to me is quite all right.
Oddly enough they hardly touch Tequila, they prefer to drink Bud light.

So why in the hell are the non-Irish getting drunk and seen wearing of the green?
Putting on" Kiss me I'm Irish" plastic hats while drinking green beer I find it most obscene.
St. Patrick's is a holy day; the true Irish spend it with their clan.
It's the wanna be Irish who piss on the day getting drunk without a plan.

It's Hallmark and their stupid cards that benefit most from this day,
And the Bar owners whose busy tills pay their tax bills in one day.
So when you see you blood shot reflection in the mirror on the 18th remember that you were warned.
You should have stayed on the porch instead of running with the big dogs, we're pro's so be for-warned.
You are really not Irish, we live our life's this way,
And remember Whiskey was created to make sure we would not conquer the world in a day.

Birthday at the Scoop Bar.

When Dennis Crowley and his wife Bev bought the Scoop Bar, it came with patrons already established as good neighbors from Saint Joe's Parrish.
No one will dispute that Dennis was a great guy but there was a side to him that you never did want to see a fight side no one would cherish.
As Dennis was one of the toughest sons of a bitch's to walk Gods earth but then again there was no nicer or friendlier a fella.
He had the heart of gold, put up with much foolishness from bar patrons, Bev and Dennis were the best, Dennis a nice guy preceded by Hell of a.

I don't know how this one tradition started, but it was put in to practice many times a year to celebrate a bar patrons birthday.
While the birthday party was rolling and the drinks were a flowing in the back of one's mind there would fear on this special day.
That one of your friends had the joy only clowns can experience, hitting the birthday boy in the face with a messy cream pie.
The tradition was kept alive every birthday for those who showed their face and I think some looked forward to the pie in the eye.

It may sound odd to the average Joe but getting pied was just an odd way for your friends to show you were in their book a true friend.
So this went off and on many times a year and it never got old, birthday plans would be shot so doing it late in the night was the trend. In one case I understood it to happen early at a Saturday Morning meeting of the Breakfast Club but this pie throw took a bad turn.
No one predicted it, it was a simple mistake and because it was done quickly the finer details were rushed and a painful lesson was learned.

I think it might have been a fella named Barrick who's birthday landed on this day so one of the bar patrons was sent to retrieve a pie.
This was the first mistake as the messenger was not to sober so in his mad dash to get to and fro he purchased a frozen Banana Cream pie.
He took the pie out of the box and for good measure drained a can of Cool Whip on top and then snuck it in and I believe he handed it to Dennis.
When the moment of surprise came about and Dennis hit Barrick as hard as a truck not knowing that the pie was frozen and unforgiving as a fence.

Barrick wore glasses, or at least he did up to that moment, as the glasses broke dead in half on his nose which collapsed like a flat tire on his face.
There was blood everywhere and you can only imagine Crowley's face when he put the puzzle together that he attempted murder in his business place.
Dennis profoundly apologized and threatened to do the same to the idiot who brought him the frozen projectile that started this fiasco.
Barrick's nose was indeed broken and needed to be reset but he was assured drinks would be waiting upon his return so to the emergency room he did go.

I was the chatter on every ones lips that night as there was live music and the bar was jumping you always felt comfortable when you were at the Scoop.
It was like you were visiting with friends in Dennis and Bev's front room and though the brick structure looked tough, inside was a well behaved group.
The main reason was the Crowley's were held in the highest respect in this niche of the mining camp during some very wild hell raising times.
The Scoop was a true juke joint and a rare neighborhood pub with its own Breakfast Club and as in life it is a true bell that has cherished chimes.

The Flats

Growing up in their Grandfathers neighborhood is not a gift that all Butte children received.
To my friends who grew up on the flats my family's stomping grounds could not be conceived.
I remember the year my world expanded when I was one of the first to attend South Central.
I looked at the pristine neighborhoods and I was amazed at how it came across pastoral.

There were no warehouses, no railroad tracks and I was not sure what else to think.
There was no corner grocery stores and I did not see one local bar for the men to drink.
There were massive lawns and smart looking houses that my new classmates live in.
I wondered where was the butcher shop, the abandoned cars and empty lots to play ball in?

To my knowledge they did not have any shanty apartment houses visited often by the police.
The streets were clean, the yards well-kept and I would not be surprised if the dogs had no fleas.
The folks who lived in the pristine neighborhoods as in mine were the salt of the earth.
Traveling to school each day in the car pools it was a good transition from our homey hearth.

I grew up down the road from the stadium and Butte High in the working class world of Saint Joes.
There were no Doctors or Lawyers in our neighborhood where disputes were settled with blows.
This daily commute from the land of labor was one of the best things to happen to me.
It gave me an understanding of the world I lived in and opened a new world for me to see.

I learned very quickly that the scenery change from my neighborhood to the land of nice homes.
Was that, just a change of scenery as I soon learned from my new friends weren't polished chrome.
I travelled down to the flats on the weekends to hang out with my new pals from the new school.
I was amazed they may have had different abodes but their Dad's knew how to use a tool.

Not all came from homes where the Dad wore a tie and Mother fluttered about in an apron.
I learned very quickly that like us siblings fought with each other then shook hands and moved on.
There was a misconception I had about the flats and I learned quickly I was totally wrong.
This new part of Butte was like my own neighborhood it was made of good people all along.

To this very day I claim solid friendship with friends from both the hill and the flats.
I am thankful I learned from my parents that we could get along unlike the dogs and cats.
It isn't the package that matters the most and be very careful not to judge one another.
We are all from one big family called Butte and we are joined like a sister and brother.

The Bar's on Fire, we need to save the Bonanini's whiskey. 1972

We had been carousing and decided to hit the world famous M and M for steak and eggs.
Else Delmoe was working the counter on the café side Muzzy was running Keno for the drunks and hags.
We had finished our meal when it hit the fan and uptown Butte became a Chinese fire drill.
Fire had taken its hold on the corners of Park and Main forever changing the skyline of the richest hill.

This is not a small shop fire or an unattended stove as this inferno quickly became a living dragon.
Every business connected to the corner would be affected by the racing fire that madly raged on.
Walking out the front door of the M and M we looked directly across Main and saw a rescue underway.
We like others waded into the smoking building to help our friends the Bonanini's get out of harm's way.

The Sportsman Bar was very much a working man's bar as it catered to the miners and gamblers.
It had a massive inventory, a liquor store at the front of saloon that had served so many Butte ramblers.
People I had seen before and others were perfect strangers walked quickly to get access to the booze.
Everything else was insured, Mr. B was a good businessman trying to salvage what he could lose.

The liquor was carried across the street and stacked behind the barriers put up by the law.
Once it was delivered we would return for another case to carry but what is important is what I saw.
To my knowledge not one bottle was looted from the uptown bars inventory as the hooch was stacked.
That says so much about all the people who helped that night hauling whiskey forth and back.

Friends and strangers went in and out of the smoke filled bar and continued for another hour or two.
The uninsured liquor inventory stayed where it was place by the volunteers who numbered a large crew.
The loss to uptown Butte was staggering yet we saw the best and trues side of the folks from Butte.

Everyone wanted to help, no one person thought of personal gain never crossing a mind to loot.

There are empty lots where these businesses' once stood and there have been many a rumor of arson.
Perhaps there is truth to the rumor as Butte suffered such a loss with the chance to rebuild long gone.
Out of this devastating loss of building and establishments that occurred on that warm Butte night,
I never saw a bit of looting though there was an opportunity and as usual Butte's folks did what's right.

The Auditor.

For the men who ran the supply side operations, on the Butte Hill when it was roaring.
 They had the Herculean task of dispersing the material used to keep copper flowing.
Hammers and screws, buckets of nails, miles of wiring does not cover the full list.
I understand some found its way to a few Butte residences, never ever being missed.

This undertaking of this scribbling is not dedicated to the actual stockpile of tools.
We shall address the unforeseen visits they had to tolerate while trying to keep cool.
No matter what went into the company, the sixth floor had an accurate accounting.
The actual numbers had to be validated for the executives, a lid Kept on the looting.

The bean counter position was created to keep track of the Sixth Floors investment.
The Auditors had to go out and beat foot in supply houses with very little lament.
The bolts had to be counted and inventory had to match the companies many items.
It was the Auditor who showed up without fanfare, stopping a leak where it stems.

The Auditors were the ghost of the company, many shop Stuarts shared the fear.
Mystery was accredited to these interloping accountants whose mission was clear.
Get in, take the count and get out and move on to spread the accounting raid.
Confusion and surprise their weapons, and it was very few friends that they made.

That description of mystery transfers from the bean counters who roamed the Pit at will.
It is needed to describe the dog name "The Auditor" and residence he had on the hill.
He resembled a Komodor, a breed with the curling ropes of hair that protected his hide.
That is just a guess as like most we never saw him, so on his history we take a dog's ride.

We look at our dog pals as they lounge on the furniture it becomes hard to compare.
This great dog survived winter on a frozen landscape that no other living being dared.
A vigil was held by this herding dog at Berkley Lake, continually looking for his lost flock.
He came and went as his pleasure, barely interacting, a fella who is not much for talk.

Some of the workers to a shine to this lone wolf and attempted to give him a meal.
He accepted their friendship toward the end of his shift, life at the pit lost its appeal.
They might have tried to cage him and if they did I am so glad their mission failed.
I admire free spirits who live with what's dealt; these survivors should never be jailed.

I understand there is a statue honoring the great watcher on George Street in Butte.
Like Bubba Maloney's picture gracing the wall at the KC, we stop and offer salute.
Butte admires tenacity and those who plow on, no matter weather or time of day,
I like the story of the Dog who lived like a monk, and he knew when to stay away.

Bobby and the Deluxe Sandwich.

Growing up between the hill and the flats ribaldry filled weekend evenings were the flavor of the day.
Juxtaposed alleyways and dimly lit passage ways roved by dimly witted drinkers spending a week's pay.
When the bottle was almost empty barkeeps would salute and bury a dead soldier in your glass.
Drinking was the primary business but the food offered only at these few bars was a special class.

Hard boiled pickled eggs and pig knuckles collect dust on the back bar when a feast was two yells away.
They were the salvation for sustenance on week end benders and in many buckets come Monday.
I speak of the wonderful creation of the Fourth Earl of Sandwich perfected at The DeLuxe Bar.
Just few blocks from my parent's front door to the Deluxe alley door there was no need for a car.

Bobby and the Deluxe made the biggest sandwiches simply they were the best of them all.
The meat was piled on bread from the Eddy's Bakery off Front Street before it became and empty hall.
There is something more than special when I recall the many Deluxe Sandwiches I had over the years.
At one time they were one fifty but no one complained as the price of the Butte Deli climbed a few tiers.

During its day the Deluxe was a must stop for card players and travelling sport teams alike.
Energized with rail road money that flooded in from the Front Street Depot added a spike.
During this time the sandwich business was a full time enterprise serving hundreds a week.
 Saturday afternoon a mixture of card players, railroaders and miners gave the population a peak.

Next door was Harry Brinks gaming and entertainment machines a matching not at all odd.
I used to watch the Brinks operation and was informed by my father Harry had more money than God.
It was a thriving and entertaining run on Front Street Brinks and the Deluxe enjoyed for decades.
The hard living ventures in the mining camp forced the gambling mecca closed from further escapades.

The Deluxe was a great Bar in our youth and it was run by a group of great guys and a woman or two.
A working man's bar that was run with a firm hand by Bobby and his well respected bartending crew.
The sandwich of legends are no longer made but I assure you a comparison to others is done quick
Anyybody from who ate a sandwich from the Deluxe compared all others using the Deluxe measuring stick.

Breaking up the parish.

I have not the time or the desire to diagnose the Catholic Church and its impact on Butte.
I do know the dynamics of the parish forever changed after the last crippling copper strike hit root.
It was downsizing in today's terminology, this last strike that took more than a pound of flesh.
The exodus from the Mining City forced families to move and seek work by beating around a new bush.

The creation of the Catholic Junior Highs changed the face of Butte for the better or worse.
Establishing football programs by flat topped Jim Patrick who asked slackers if they carried a purse.
Grade schools became more crowded and more Nuns decided Kansas was not such a bad place.
I was good lemming and followed the others to meld into the crowd and be just another face.

Although it remained a powerhouse the Church got its clocks cleaned by the Anaconda Company.
When mining was good tithing was better and the Arch Diocese of Helena had gravitas politically.
Active schools became surplus property and the pecuniary Diocese coat tails became week.
As the metamorphous continued it took some adjustment yet the future did not appear so bleak.

It needs to be stated I have not darkened a Butte church doorway in well over a decade,
I am a recovering Catholic but I am not a bully so I keep quiet when it comes to the abuse charade.
I am not out to pontificate but I am simply recalling how the last strike was such a brutal blow.
The Butte Catholic Church had their knees weakened when the Company pulled the plug on the show.

I try to calibrate how Butte is doing from a distance and I see the abandoned buildings posted.
I hear that parish mass now takes in a bigger territory and the attendance has downhill coasted.
When I did visit the Mining City I always walked and took my own inventory of the Catholic Church.
And like all the hits that Butte took over decades by the company the Catholics are still in a lurch.

Brings tears to a set of Glass Eyes.

Growing up the youngest of six boys has its benefits and more than a few drawbacks.
I had a hell of a security force in place with my brothers from any type of attacks.
There were some negative aspects of being the pup in an all boy large Irish clan.
It seemed to me I never had to shop for clothes, as I got my brothers second hand.

I look back at those days and I realize that the McGinley boys came out just fine.
Like an aboriginal tribe lost from civilization we had no idea of the poverty line.
My parents, I now know did without more than I realized as they kept sacrifice quiet.
That and the fact all our neighborhood families had budgets that were just as tight.

We did not buy new bikes to ride in the summer they were hand built in the garage.
Frames and tires were salvaged from around town and the collection got very large.
We attended the neighborhood Catholic school so salt and pepper pants were worn.
God help you if you wore then after school when rough housing and if they got torn.

I am a witness to what hard times are made of as I was around during copper strikes.
I was young and concerned about playing; the hardship was kept away from us tikes.
What made the times almost bearable was that the hard times hit the entire town.
We learned early not to judge what others did not have or upon them to look down.

I was seven or eight and the first Copper Strike I can remember hit the mining camp.
Striking teamsters manned picket lines for a day earning the price of a postage stamp.
I will never understand how mortgages were paid and food made its way to the table.
We were told the strikes were important for men's rights and to be healthy and able.

The bars had drinking tabs and the neighborhood taverns became local union headquarters.
The strike went on for many hard months as the Company and Union Leaders did barter.
Families pulled resources and held each other up and church parishes became stronger.
When meals are too few and winter clothes are needed luxuries are needed no longer.

It was the winter of the strike that I still keep fresh in my mind, even until this day.
It was Christmas supplemented by the unions and for gifts of choice children did pray.
I myself was fortunate as my hard working Dad was steadily employed as a fireman.
I am embarrassed to relate my behavior that December but it became a part of life's plan.

It was a special Christmas for me, more so than some others, and I had the world by the tail.
I tore into my presents seeking out a GI Joe Astronaut figure but alas it was to no avail.
The one gift I wanted so much and mentioned daily to Santa was nowhere to be found.
I got as pissed as a hornet squirted with a hose, my temper and bitching had no bounds.

The misbehavior did not last too long as my Mom and Dad had enough of my shit.
I had my sorry ass planted at the kitchen table and was firmly told my fussing to quit.
I started to appeal in my defense of the hardship in between my sobs and cries.
My Mom told me my story was touching; it could bring tears to a set of glass eyes.

I use that phrase often in life and I now understand what comes with the Irish saying.
You cannot swing a dead cat without hit another who suffers more and I should be praying.
Some look at the tough times in life and they carry it with them wherever they go.
I would like to believe I put this self-serving attitude with powder to hell it will blow.

There are some who are not as fortunate as I; they have had life handed to them on a plate.
Like other Butte Rats who learned to do with out and be thankful for what's in our fate.
My Mom and Dad never lied to me and today I know those times did make me strong.
It is because of the strikes and knowing what is a true gift that I am able to get along.

I still get a chuckle when I think of the life changing phrase "Tears to a set of glass eyes."
That being selfish is a wish in one hand and shit in the other and see what the combo will buy.
In the reflection of time I now take these lessons with me wherever I may stand.
I am thankful for Butte and the lessons and friends, for my life joys are truly quite grand.

Scooping out Prayers with a butter knife.

We all got dragged in to some sort of service that our parents deemed we would be worthy to execute.
I am not talking about household chores or shoveling snow, but special duties that made us astute.
Even though it was pointed out to us at the time, that the activity was a way to better ones self.
It does not hit us, until we reflect on the meaning of the work and put selfishness on the shelf.

One special task that was performed by me and my brothers involved a morning job that took an hour.
My Dad was dedicated to the Parrish of St. Joes up until he no longer run on his own power.
Now I realize the jon was not that bad, we used old butter knifes to scrape out the old votive candles.

Once the candle was spent it was replaced with another for another prayer to be handled.

I was thinking of this and I now know what the lesson was as we reloaded the glass urns of prayer.
It is does good to volunteer ones time to be of service to others and yet I found yet another layer.
Through the years my brothers and I must have replaced thousands of the candles over the decades.
And I think about all the prayers we handled over the years and to this sunny story arrives some shade.

I wonder how many parishioners used there last dollar to light a candle in times when there was none.
I recall some families who we wondered how they survived and to faith was when they would run.
Those thousands of candles that we scraped away after it had burned and run its course.
That pesky job now has a different meaning to me on what is worth for holding remorse.

I think of the prayers that were made for injured miners or that way ward child who went astray.
I keep that lesson close to me as I had the reaffirmation that when it's bad, it's time to pray.
I have tried to research the reason why candles are lit and it goes forever back in measured time.
I did find one thing as I gave it some thought and it comes to me as a resonate chime.

Some say you are wasting your efforts praying to a God that does not listen or even exist.
That lighting a candle is a pagan act of worship worthless as praying to an eclipse.
To those good folks I harbor no ill feelings and perhaps they would change their mind.
It is better to light a candle than curse the darkness works like a prayer every time.

Puppet Head.

He is standing next to Mickey who just finds it impossible to stop bragging about a red headed whore.
The trouble is he is going to be mucking next to him with hours more of his red light stories in store.
Last week's dirt is captured in his rubbing shirt collar; there are is no scent of home where he stands.
It is the life he had chosen in to make his fortune, now he is moving raw copper ore with his hands.

The whistle screams the end of shift and the Gallows poppet head powers up to haul the miners.
Last smokes are had, nips of pocket whiskey taken and a last check of his equipment is in order.
The lot of men quietly shuffle in boots greased with bacon drippings for the water proofing.
It mattered not was used to water proof boots as they would end up sloppy wet and chaffing.

The cage door slams open and the first shift pours out in time to see the Big Sky in light.
The last hours have been spent in tunnels thousands of feet underground and out of sight.
The cage is clear and the first dozen men load up to take the elevator to Bill Clark's hell.
Packed into the metal cage like liquor in the case the operator gives the "All clear!" yell.

Powerful electric engines jump to life from the current carried on the wires they mined.
The clutch engages, the gear wheel throws a spark as the cage and its charges descend.
The multiple levels wiz by as sheltered air blasts into the cage pushed by large fans.
Minutes later after twelve hundred foot drop in the earth, the immigrant trolley lands.

Hundreds and thousands of men and mining livestock have been pushed underground.
The poppet head, called the Puppet head for the lines it controls as it rolls up and down.
 The few inches of metal wound together for strength are at the puppeteer's control.
Great care given to this life line and cage as it daily carried hundreds of brave souls.

I am not sure of you but I can only imagining riding this freight train straight down.
Keeping up good spirits all the while doing back breaking work, to me it astounds.
When you remember over two thousand men died in order to bring up the ore.
 It is hard to bitch about my troubles today, I am quite sure they would find me a bore.

Walking uphill both ways to get to school, we have all heard the description before.
I chuckled at the absurdity of the two hill walk but I now see the message under score.
My friends today share the same type of story with our children as we try to guide.
The next time and older person tells me a story, I will let my false pride step aside.

Under today's laws the mining operations of the Company would surely be shut down.
We have heard of the many deaths in the mines but no injury list could be found.
I have admitted it before, I will admit it again compared to these men I'm a slouch.
I admire their spirit and determination and for their bold courage I can only vouch.

I never knew of my families hardships, like good Irish there was no time for bitching.
I read of their Journey on steamers and came across the ocean for a new life searching.
No matter what I may go through I will never come close to their living in hard time.
I pull together that fight that was bred in me and remember living hard is no crime.

The Anselmo, the Orphan Girl, the Travona, the Original, the Steward, the Lexington, the Mountain Con, the Kelley, the Belmont, the Bell, the Granite Mountain, and the Badger.

Butte Tough.

Take a trip with me down to the corner where anger intersects with bad luck
It's where one's metal is tested, life changing choices are made and there's no passing the buck.
It's where a mirror is held up while the world watches to see how you handle the news.
Your response is unexpected to those who know not your heritage; there was no singing the blues.

Look at the simple word "Tough" and all that is enduring and substantial jumps to the front of one's mind.
Those words fall short when it comes to this verbiage, for "Butte Tough" is its own special kind.
True those who mined rock and lived for the moment they were the truest image of strength.
Yet Butte owns a rare breed of tough of which there are no boundaries, no width nor length.

My mother Sam was "Butte Tough" though just five feet tall her strengths came from what she went through.
"Make the best with what you have" were her teachings to her boys of what is "Butte Tough" still stands true.
When you ask "Butte Tough" how they're feeling when you know they are knocking on deaths front door,
"Fine" is the answer then the conversation is steered to blessings bestowed and life's gifts galore.

To the outsider and interlopers into Butte traditions and what separates "Butte Tough" from the rest.
They may think it means drinking and brawling but that is truly not "Butte Tough" at its best.
"Butte Tough" is Bubba Maloney, his passing to early from us all was a tough break.
"Butte Tough" came out in true Bubba form; he said "Fuck cancer" and threw his own wake.

"Butte Tough" is not how you handle the cold or how many beers that you drank.
"Butte Tough" makes going through tough times look easy and remembering the good Lord to thank.
"Butte Tough" does not react with vengeance when no one person would blame you if you took.
Like Leo McCarthy getting "Butte Tough" with Mariah's Challenge, he faced hells gate and it shook.

Mike Mansfield was one of our nations great Senators born and raised in Butte years ago.
The Senator knew "Butte Tough" as he lived serving others, a path we all should go.
My Dad Jack was "Butte Tough" for decades he fought fires and his public service of which we are proud.
His Butte Tough was not found hanging in the bars, his forty years of service to St. Joe's Parrish speaks loud.

"Butte Tough" is dusting yourself off before you are even steady on your feet.
It is using all the anger inside you to metamorphous a gifting life that is never fully complete.
"Butte Tough" comes about through prayers not asking "Why" but "What can I do?"
"Butte Tough" comes out when others gave up. "Butte Tough" is me and you.

Sargent Maurice Mulcahy

The summer's In Butte were a small boys great days, the Mining City had much to offer.
For the young entrepreneurs it meant staying out late shining shoes to put coins in their coffer.
There was great sand piles behind the Civic Center on which you could run and jump off.
Sleep outs in back yards, raiding neighbor's gardens and sneaking a smoke no matter the cough.

Of course some hooliganism was bound to take place the lad's free spirits demanded relief.
In the winter it was throwing snow balls at cars, but with summer it turned a new leaf.
The boundaries lifted with warm weather and in expanded territories the fella's freely did roam.
It meant visits to Clarks Park and Silver Bows Shit Creek and the Columbia Gardens were a second home.

But no matter the offerings mischievous behavior took root and trouble makers found a new heaven.
And that is the core of this tale, with Jerry Riordan, he is a few years older than my dear brother Kevin.
It was a hot summer night and I ran into Jerry Riordan in the alley behind the Deluxe Bar.
We both were quite bored looking for action but we did not wish to wonder too far.

We crossed over Front Street right by the Depot and we soon were wandering on the train tracks.
We put down some pennies on the rail to be run over by the train to check we would have to back track.
We found rail road spikes and a workers lunch box, and some broken glass from a rail switcher
A railroad cop yelled at us to leave the rail yard Jerry yelled he should go fuck his Sister.

We ran further into the yard and came upon a wall of windows for the great locomotives shed.
We stood still for a moment then notice the rocks, various projectiles on the tracks bed.
We each picked up a rock and let it set sail, the breaking glass sound filled us with glee.
Before the second round launched we saw a cop car and immediately we had to flee.

Jerry Riordan ran North and I headed due west to my parents safety was the only thought I had.
But I had to shake the cops, so I used the labyrinth of the alleys before I made it to my folk's pad.
I came around the corner and my greatest fear hit, the cop car was parked in front of my house.
I knew I had nowhere to run, the cops were the cat and I was the idiot mouse.

My Dad met me at the door pissed as a hornet whose nest had been attacked and disturbed.
I figured if I could keep my cool this could blow over no matter how badly my Dad was perturbed.
I walked in the front door and headed for the kitchen and heard the unmistakable laugh.
It was Sargent Maurice Mulcahy a good friend of the family, a shepherd with a firm staff.

To this day I don't know what happened I have reviewed this scenario as much as I can.
I yelled "I wasn't there and neither was Jerry Riordan." Being a hoodlum was no long the plan.
Maurice broke out laughing, my dad cracked a smile and my Mom stopped being a cook.
Maurice said "Paddy you're not a good criminal, and I believe you will never make it as a crook".

My unsolicited confession probably saved my ass, humor can turn things around.
And Maurice let it ride this time, knowing my Dad's punishment would surely be sound.
Maurice did visit Jerry's parents, and for his prank he got grounded for a full week.
For a full month he wanted to kick my ass, through the neighborhood I had to sneak.

Shit Creek.

To the north of Winston Salem outside of Walnut Cove is a part of the world locals call "The Dan"
I know a couple fellas from that part of the planet and fly fishing and floating are grand.
I enjoyed my travels into the mid-west and in Wisconsin on the river they have "The Dells."
Limestone walls carved away over centuries, offset beauty in a wonderful place to dwell.

In Montana, Missoula has the River and Billings and Great Falls share in same gift of natural wealth.
In Butte we had our special tributary "Shit Creek" to go near it was piss poor for your health.
It is not much of a nick name for the headwaters of the Clark Fork River but it comes honest to the name.
As usual when you are dealing with a wrong to the people of Butte the Company carries the shame.

There were numerous ways to traverse the poison waters laced with arsenic and lead.
There were cross water lines that traversed Shit Creek that we kids maneuvered with dread.
It was always a wasteland and people treated it so on the banks were abandoned machines.
The closest I got near it was no more than a few feet for fear a joker I'm with might think I was to clean.

I tossed rocks, sticks, radiators, wheels, tires, a dead cat and an automobile door into the abyss.
I was guilty as everyone for who ever thought that Shit Creek would make it on the clean water list.
It has been said the creek caused a high incident of cancer and perhaps it did, but not only the human kind.
It was perpetrated by a generation of heathens who scarred the land then played clueless feigning an eye of the blind.

So you have this stretch of poison water running through the middle of the indigenous population.
It kills all vegetation, a buzzard wouldn't drink it and we know the name of who caused this stagnation.
It is times such as these that I wish Atlantic Richfield treated Butte residents like Eskimo's when it comes to pay.
I think every living Butte resident should get a thousand bucks from AR for having to put up with Shit Creek in past day.

Sainted McQueen.

The societal rule of "hate the sin not the sinner" is the finding of the court for story clarity.
It takes on a second tone of one being forced to bring down a deity, for a few men's prosperity.
This duty required a commitment to an employer one that calls for silent performance of duty.
It tears at your very core, and in your heart it is an atrocity to bring the end of a small city.

When attacking an opponent and seizing a city the first thing guerilla's take is communication.
When a corporation seizes a city they destroy a community's past, advancing their exploitation.
There is no other way to look at their actions outside the basic rules of bare knuckle boxing.
It can get brutal but one rule that is never broken is a cheap shot during the shellacking.

To those who observed the burying of the Holy Savior Church this was more than a dirty trick.
It was more than a head butt cut, as that can be handled by a good cut man and his styptic stick.
This was below the belt and swiftly done in order disable the victim, forcing the end of the fight.
They took a village with roots deeper than others and stole it away like a thief in the night.

I did not attend the church but like all other Butte churches its sacred community ran deep.
They buried a structure was the terms used on the Sixth Floor, committed with lightning speed.
In the accounting by The Company this was nothing more than a small parcel of all their land.
It was weddings and magnificent receptions and celebrations they could never understand.

To the families of McQueen this had to be seen as a final bullet behind the ear to a beloved animal.
We seem to grieve more for the innocent that are destroyed and pilfered not the sole individual.
I can only imagine what that was like for the first generation settlers to see this abomination occur.
I have witnessed losses, yet I believe McQueen has experienced a loss that makes mine demure.

With the loss of the hallmarks like the church, the McQueen community folk did the best thing.
They kept their neighborhoods and friend in their hearts, married to memories which needed no ring.
It can be compared to a war zone powered by eminent domain that brought McQueen to its knees.
While kneeling they prayed and then stood up to start again, knowing they paid the highest of fees.

What is written in stone from the fall of McQueen is how all of the citizens carried the good attitude.
They had the houses they lived in for generations bought, and approached life with a joyful mood.
You meet a person or family which has its roots and memories in place with the sainted McQueen.
The Company may have taken McQueen's churches, but their toughness and grace is always seen.

Special place in hell. (The Columbia Gardens)

There is one man who walked this earth who had to come up with the terrible plan.
He awoke one morning looked out his window and decided to increase hell's span.
He showered and shaved as he always did and then headed to work out his front door.
All the way to work he began to smirk as he decided the Columbia Gardens would be no more.

It was 1973 when the powers to be, voted the gates to heaven should close forever.
Yet the demise of the Gardens began in an office behind the mind of evil and so clever.
Like a secret handshake or hidden password the shuttering of the Gardens stayed quiet.
To hell with the people and this place of beauty if they knew it could mean a riot.

These corporate men did not look at smiles or the joys this touch of Eden brought.
There was copper to mine, corporate growth to have and selfish profits to be sought.
The Proms, the Festivities and family gatherings so many with no time to mention,
Matter nothing to the men of numbers, their only concern to not gather attention.

The plan was made and elation swept the top floors of The Anaconda Company Corporation.
They'll continue to carve and scar the city of copper and its mile high elevation.
The wooden water tower where many a first kiss and golden memories were made,
Was leveled and then leached of its beauty, the first victim of this unholy raid.

The cowboy swings no longer moved and the bi-plane ride was soon disassembled.
The flowers and gardens allowed to perish the spirit of youth no longer rambled.
The main pavilion and the roller coaster were decommissioned not but skeletons remained.
This is not what the Copper King had envisioned when the Gardens idea was first entertained.

At the turn of the century William Clark bought the land but not for a material gains.
He bought it for the children of Butte in which to play and escape their life's pains.
For all the citizens it became a back yard, nature's great cathedral they attended.
It was grace, it was heaven, it became a haven where a hard life could suspended.

Decades have passed since the corporate fools and greed put this grand lady of the Rockies down.
As each year passes so do the memories of what was true beauty in the rough copper town.
I close my eyes and I can smell the gardens and feel the creaks of the boarded walk way.
Feel the jolt of the penny shock machine, we rode the bus for free on children's day.

Being Butte there were keggers held in valleys but it was the family picnics I remember the most.
There was the yellow playhouse we all visited and of course the roller on which we did coast.
The Merry Go Round still plays the music of magical and sun filled Saturdays well spent.
My parent danced in the Pavillion, all memories all so golden and full of rewarded content.

And for the dirty bastards who decided to mine there I hope they are nothing but a haunted ghost.
May they wandered the abandoned halls of the corporate false castles with an empty glass to toast,
I am usually more moderate in my temper these days, especially since I no longer drink.
But those who robbed Butte of the gardens, they have a special place in hell, or so I'd like to think.

Copper Strikes.

My dad Jack was a Butte Fireman which kept him employed when The Company did rule.
For a while it seemed that burning buildings in uptown was a crude form of urban renewal.
Though I was a lad when the copper strikes hit Butte it affected us but was not all consuming
It was the talk of the city and it rumbled through our lives copper was no longer booming.

I was ten years old when the strike of 67 brought mining to halt and made many Butte families stronger.
Most believed the importance of the miners would bring quick resolve but it went for months and longer.
I was impossible not to know at least one family who took a beating and suffered because of the strike.
Father's use to providing well for their families walked picket lines in an unending circular hike.

One thing I was told in my early age that only a few enjoyed the wealth at the working man's blight.
The truth was finally being made aware that a decent living in copper could disappear overnight.
These strikes seemed predetermined as the Company fought to keep corporate profits flowing.
They closed their eyes to the suffering as the foundation of the working man's finance began crumbling.

As we grew up in these times it seemed no force could tear apart the family or Butte itself,
Yet like an Uncle who suffered and injury who was never "quite right" and not "his old self"
The strafing's of those months not working and miners meeting in bars to bitch and complain.
 Its mark on the community and weakened the knees of the unions a Company held in disdain.

The children of those difficult times seem to have scattered yet their shadows and stories remain.
No one child of a Company worker can help themselves not to recall the loss and pain.
It became a tool on which to measure success and gave many the ability to do without.
The strike may have started the downfall of mining but that is not what this discussion is about.

Butte still stands and is a symbol to others that if your heart is good you will always survive.
Butte tough became a part of each being making many wanting to live and not just survive.
Butte dusted itself off from the scrap and though many did move to leave mining behind.
Every one of those folks and their children share the true meaning of Butte Tough in their mind.

Pissing in a radiator.

It was a magnificent day on the Big Hole River and the float trip could not have gone better.
The rules of the river including raft etiquette were in firm place when it came to beer cans and litter.
The fishing was not the best but the beer was as we used a raft cooler as big as a coffin.
The raft held the six of us explorers just fine as we floated, drank and spent a day laughing.

My brother Kevin and I took his Blazer as the lead car and carried the needed supplies.
The sandwiches with us reflected good intentions for beer was breakfast in the Big Sky.
Morning services were held in each saloon if it shared any co-ordinates with the river.
Our lives were to see only what was in front of us not hardships or failure of liver.

The river trip ended as we broke down the raft and we made our plans for the night.
It all came down to how we would feel or not feel if bar drinks would fuel the night flight.
We climbed back into the vehicles sun burned and satisfied and surely feeling no pain.
We started headed toward the Wise River Club then what happened is hard to explain.

My brother got false courage and the fire to explore the Great Divide on the way home.
Within a matter of minutes the Blazer was headed on a path a goat would never roam.
The Blazer took a bump and a smack and for a bit we seemed to be at a 45 angle degree,
We came to rest steam was blasting out of the hood resting against the trunk of a tree.

After some of my more harrowing experiences in my drinking years I kept only one motto.
No matter what happens as long as I am still in Montana it's a jam I can get out of.
There was no such thing as a cell phone and where we were wrecked not even a field shed.
When we got out of the Blazer to survey the damage I wanted to punch my brother in the head.

We had a cracked radiator and to add to the fun a rock had puncture a hole in the gas tank.
A half tank of fuel running down the middle of this path so I made sure to Kev I said "Thanks"
I have to give my brother credit for without pause he made a plug with his shirt and a stick.
Our next problem was a draining radiator and no source of water, not even a trickling crick.

We had the cooler that was holding some water so we poured it in after using some JB Weld.
By the time the water circulated around the block we were all amazed that the patch still held.
We were still short of the coolant we needed to get back to the Mining City with no overheating.
I looked at my brother whose mind was conceiving a fix to his vehicle and avoiding a beating.

We had the idea we would get back to Butte and then an emergency motor flush would be done.
It was then we decided it would be best to filter the beer through our bodies while having a little fun.
The patch in the gas tank held quite well while we drank the beer and collected natures coolant.
We made it to the Wise River Club running on piss and beer and for work not one of us was truant.

Orbit and OXO.

I met up with OXO at the Speedway Bar Tony Valpondo was cooking up a storm in the Cantina.
We had dinner at the bar libations were had and for dessert some product from Peru or Argentina.
We took off from the bar in OXO's Corvette as he told me he was Hans Solo in The Millennium Falcon.
We headed out for a serious evening of great carousing and any good times to be found.

OXO's brother Dave "Orbit" Corbett was also around for those days or more accurately the nights.
When I think of the Corbett's I cannot help but smile whose sheer genius was the brightest of lights.
Some of the projects the brothers undertook can be listed among Mining City urban legends.
The mirrored vehicles of OXO to Orbit growing trees in abandoned mines for environmental amends.

I heard one story how the two decided that the Wright Brothers legend needed a challenge.
A hang glider was built and Orbit was designated the test pilot controlling with a flange.
There is a video many have seen it is penguins following a light with total head synchronization.
To describe the flight, Orbit went up and back down the crowd's heads in sync for the demolition.

OXO designed Evel Knievels first mansion being a modern wizard his real calling was Architecture.
If you missed out on the tour of his house on Timber Butte it was a castle as comfy as a favorite chair.
There was a huge bird origami suspended inside and tie collection sewn together as a tapestry.
It had the original use of solar energy in the state in a building that was a big part of Butte's history.

I had great times with the brothers and to be honest Dave had what the Irish call a "glorious thirst.
I have a feeling that habit was part of his early demise he won't be the last and he wasn't the first.
This great Butte family left the earth very quickly in a matter of a few years they were all gone.
It is sad to write that OXO's collection of art and design was lost in fire and accidental wrong.

It was the end of the building and all of OXO's fine work but let's move past this awful mistake.
Before the fire Orbit had great plans to share his brother's creation and refused money to take.
OXO and Dave gave gifts to the city including art work for Lake Berkley and Knievel Days.
Though they may not be next to you on a barstool, their spirit and genius will always stay.

Painting the dog.

There is a secret society among the Butte males, the Skull and Bones of Archie and Jughead sodality.
How the society formed no one knows nor will any willingly admit any membership to the sorority.
There is the possibility you might hear of the tale of misdemeanor entrance activity to this union.
You would have to be old as the story is told at only at a Butte Central or Butte High class reunion.

I am sworn to secrecy again as I recall the happenings and consuming of many libations.
That and the fact it is no longer done and I am sure no longer considered with the statute of limitations.
The undertaking of the task started innocent enough with a few cohorts who shall remain unnamed.
It starts with a bathroom discussion while sneaking a smoke and ended with me getting maimed.

I am the youngest of six boys so you can imagine the tales I have heard from my mischievous brothers,
Being Maroons in every sense there was a dislike of Bulldogs and unkind words said of their Mothers.
To beat the cross town rivals, well not really cross town they were right down the hill off Main Street.
But to beat the Bulldogs in any and all endeavors was all we could sleep, drink and eat.

A rowdy tradition for the mining city came after summer and the beginning of fall football season.
The gladiators would battle at Naranche Stadium and bragging rights became part of the reason.
But a few of us bright lads decided to once again pick up the torch and be an entry in the historic log.
We would steal paint from our parents, jump the barbed wire fence and hurl the paint on the dog.

We remembered years of past when attending the game and walking down the west end of the field
We walked down where the hooligan's roamed ground level for war where most would not yield.
Then the vandalism seen on the painted Bulldog seemed to strike a note of revenge and false hate.
And for some reason why I can never explain we would repeat the foul deed in night so late.

A Sunday night was chosen, it was quiet on the Sabbath our chances of getting caught quite small.
We would pilfer the paint from our dad's home stash just samples sure to not take it all.
Gerber jars were the chosen projectiles we would prepare them the park by Charlie Judds.
We would hop the barbed wire fence go under the bleachers then rest and drink a few suds.

The actual attack would take a minute or so and we reminded ourselves to keep things down.
If I get caught doing this act I would make the front page described as being a clown.
It would be worth the risk, the glory intoxicating and oh so sweet revenge.
For an unknown imagined wrong doing that when I reflect it still makes me cringe.

So we piled into a car and made the rounds picking up supplies and our soldiers of misfortune.
We had trouble on our minds, vandalism in our heart and a painting on which to lay ruin.
We arrived behind Judd's and unloaded the car and scampered for the fence running double.
But an accident occurred as we attempted to clear the fence which we learned saved us from trouble.

I am far from athletic but my years of playing forty miles kept me in good climbing shape.
But escaping from prison would not be my forte as old barbed wire foiled me as an ape.
I got to the top I was to be the first over and the rest they would climb over and follow.
What we did not expect was me getting caught on said fence like a criminal hung on the gallow.

I tore open my shin, put in quite a deep gash and the blood shed forced the mission to abort.
So there I hung there like a cat in a tree hoping not to get arrested and brought to justice court.
A flash of headlights sent all but one of my fellow shenanigan makers scrambling for the dark.
I finally got off the fence and with the help of a pal, limped away leaving a trail of blood to Vet's park.

The weapons abandoned and much discussion was had on what was to be our next move of chance.
I was told by the driver my bleeding had to stop his Dad's car was not Tucker McGree's ambulance.
So at the emergency room I had to go get stiches in my shin our troubled journey ended that night,
I look at the scar to this day and remember that evening and know God kept us walking the path that is right

Pastie Day

There is major participant in the settling of the mining camp that is long ignored and taken for granted.
The industrialized world was made in part with immigrants and the potato's they brought then planted.
Butte had its own binder of industry packed away in the buckets of the men who mined underground,
With preparations asking carrots be cut to the size of a Cornish woman's digit the recipe proved to be sound.

Philly may have the working man's Cheese Steak but next to the Pastie it is nothing but a crock.
The Pastie, the meal of a miner, is a made with all the ingredients for the men who moved rock.
From the trays of the small pasties made for weddings to Mom's extra batch tucked in the home.
Butte needs to acknowledge this staple of the citizen for the Pastie does not far from Butte roam.

I have my Mom's directions that she gave me over the phone, making a Pastie brings a bit of Butte back.
I cannot recall a sad event or perhaps some bad news where a Pastie was an integral part of the track.
The Pastie is associated with all that is good, there is no such thing as eating a bad one.
Store bought Pasties my Mom called them "Good Friday'sl" as when it came to meat was none.

Some traditions call for fine china to be used or perhaps a special bottle of wine is chosen.
I believe that everyone from Butte brings tradition alive with pasties by the dozen.
Not one soul who rears from Butte can deny the affection for the all in one meal.
It is just one delicious fact of how Butte was settled and became the real deal.

I believe a parade should be had and pasties should be served to all by the hundred.
A proclamation should be made and a declaration sealed for the base of the kindred.
For many acknowledge that to feel at home nothing captures it like the fresh baked delight.
I miss them, I am headed to the kitchen, for I will have sweet memories and a Pastie tonight.

Gamer's Honest till.

When I was doing afternoons at KXLF I enjoyed the hours of the lenient air shift.
It meant rolling into work about noon and getting out in time for a few suds to lift.
I had many pals in the music business that would swing by when they were passing through,
Being a good host I enjoyed giving them a tour of Butte and hitting the M and M after two.

The next day arrived and they had to be on the road good and early with miles of travel ahead.
It is important after closing down Maloney's to grab some breakfast to straighten out your head.
The most important meal of the day could be found at the Four B's or the standby Martha's Café.
If the opportunity was available and time was not important I liked to add a tale to their stay.

I would have them follow me uptown and we would have our morning meal at Gamer's on Park.
This important qualification is needed to be made as my pal Paul Cote kept it from going dark,
In this story our hero is man who was one of Buttes many eccentric and good hearted men.
How he ran his business and more explicitly his cash till is a story worth telling again.

I write about Carl the long time proprietor of one of Buttes longest running establishments.
Carl never seemed to have a bad morning and he did his best to make his patrons content.
He greeted all with "Good Morning" and if he knew your family he inquired of health by name,
Carl was an institution and always will be, when he moved on to cater for God it was a shame.

As I get back to the story and why I brought the interlopers to this comfortable spot.
It wasn't the food although delicious it was, the point of the visit was talked all about.
Once the meal was had and the waitress was tipped we prepared to go separate ways,
The cash register was where you stopped to pay and this is when my guests became amazed.

I took the ticket for the meal and then I the patron went and opened up the cash drawer.
Carl did not run up and ask "What in the hell are you doing?" as I worked on his cash store.
Carl allowed just about everyone who was a regular diner to take care of their own bill.
Many times as I opened the cash drawer Carl would wave goodbye unconcerned of the till.

The looks on my pal's faces made me wish I had a camera to capture their mugs for posterity.
They had all heard and experienced self-serve situations but non like this in the Mining City.
Being polite I never did ask Carl if his till was ever short but I am sure he was never robbed.
The act of purposeful faith passed on to those who at Gamer's gathered to hob knob.

Many Gamer's regulars such as Kevin Shannon and Harp Cote helped themselves paying their tab.
Carl to some came off as a bit of a kook but they were just busy bodies needing a topic to blab.
Harps son Paul wisely ended the practice when he took the helm to reestablish the café.
Yet I have to tell you that never in my travels have I never met another Carl and his odd way to pay.

Fourth of July Lie

It was ten o'clock on the holiday, humid and the corner of his world is at peace.
Not one fire cracker had been ignited; his ridged outlook had a razor sharp crease.
No confetti littered his driveway the shattered clothing of the explosive device.
There were no abandoned roman candles; the lack of burned pavement is nice.

It was good there were no children around; they're noisy and little pests.
And let's not forget the relatives from out of town, nothing but irritating insects.
This frozen pizza will do just fine for dinner, not a fan of barbeque and cold beer.
Eating alone is OK on this Holiday he really did not want to be with any one near.

He slept well or as good as could be and the calm quiet night settled his nerves.
He was content to on being alone today and not watching a parade from a curb. .
The last thing he needed for his bad neck was to be gawking at fireworks in the sky.
The travel would be hell; it was out of the way, God knows he hates to fly.

He stretched and yawned as he looked over his backyard and realized it was a lie.
He was missing his home and knew he had to see it one more time before his time slipped bye.
His convenient misinformation no longer worked covering the hard truth with pity's soot.
It would take place next year, he promised himself, and he had to get home to Butte.

There had been a life of denial on what the Mining City has meant in his life.
He realized his fond memories of Butte over rode his imagined trouble and strife.
There was no longer the empty blame he had worn on his soul as a thorny crown.
His salvation and need to reconcile his life would be found in the mining town.

The decision was made and a peace settled in as he verified the plan.
He would have to visit his home of his childhood to become a better man.
His denial of past errors no longer took place as he realized the task at hand.
You can never go home is not a sound thought when you're from Montana's Ireland.

Drinking a ditch.

I was new to the world having never left Butte outside of the occasional in state vacation.
After leaving the nest, my first stop was Minneapolis via the Front Street train station.
I thought to myself what an adventurous life laid ahead as I left my home and Butte far behind.
Little did I know that Butte and its customs would travel with me forever etched on my mind.

I am not being judgmental for I was taught to accept all races and to learn about what others spoke.
Yet I was taken aback by the diversity of the Twin Cities, curious indeed was this young Irish bloke.
Growing up in Butte I heard of the Chinese of days past and Europe where most families came from.
It seemed the only African Americans I saw in Butte were tourists; on the other races I was quite dumb.

I had numerous questions on the on how the world worked outside the confines of the Mining City.
I made a few errors; I committed social faux paux, nothing too serious that would require a friend's pity.
I was amazed to find out that many heard of a Shepard's pie but had no knowledge of the Pasty.
I soon realized that the rest of the world had no idea of Butte and on drinking they seemed rusty.

I was not of legal age to be drinking yet being from Butte how I learned how to gain entrance to a bar.
Armed with my brothers ID the family resemblance worked with the doormen in all cities near and afar.
I was a beer drinker but being Irish I had a taste for "The water of life" the delightful friend whiskey.
I went to see Willy Nelson at club and when bellied up to order the communications became iffy.

I did not order a Mai Tai or a screwdriver holding on to my Butte lifestyle I ordered a whiskey ditch.
The bartender looked at me as if I was from Mars and his befuddled head he gave a quick itch.
"Never heard of it" he said and he asked me if there was something else I would like to stifle my thirst.
I then told him the drink was not complicated and I proceeded to tell him he needed the whiskey first.

I told him to put a couple fingers of the tan elixir in the glass and make sure it had a touch of ice.
I told him to add a splash of water from the bar gun and the told him a splash of 7 Up would be nice.
He put the drink together and before he took the money he asked me from where I did hale.
I told him Montana, specifically Butte and then I told him of miners who drank beer from a pail.

The conversation continued on the way people order libations and I realized my Butte drink was special.
We discussed how the drink got tagged with the name from the cowboys coming in off the cow trail.
We hypothesized that the only way to soften whiskey was to use the available water that was on hand.
 I realized at that moment was the drink's name was unusual as is Butte is to other parts of this land.

My travels continued for many decades and I assure you my shadow darkened many saloon doors.
I cannot keep track the many times I baffled bartenders when asking for a ditch to be poured.
The ordering of a simple Butte drink opened many conversations and broke the ice, pardon the pun.
I learned back then what I still know true to this day Butte is and always will be a great place to be from.

He's OK, He's from Butte.

I live in North Carolina these days, I moved here in the 90's to be with my kid's and to work in radio.
Here in the South many cling to their rebel flags and redneck heritage for some it is all they know.
I did my radio show at different stations throughout the Old Dominion never the same format,
I enjoyed each and every place I have lived in my gypsy years yet there is one important fact.

I attended social events where someone would hear my voice and ask "Where ya'll from?"
I would tell them Montana, specifically Butte and I was no longer viewed as a Yankee bum.
If you are from north of the Mason Dixon line you might want to leave and just turn around.
But if you're from the west you are a welcomed guest to stay un the South's holy ground.

As the inquisition turned into a conversation once they learned I was not a carpet bagger.
I would always be asked about did we still ride horses and fight each other with a dagger.
I would explain horses they did indeed ride but the days of Indian fighting were long gone.
That is unless you did your drinking on the Reservation which wouldn't last that long.

Inevitably the backyard visit would turn to growing up in the mountains and specifically Butte,
No matter who I was speaking with I would be amazed that many knew of the town of my youth.
Sure Evel Knievel was the ambassador that most southerners recall when thinking of the Mining City.
Yet there were many who knew of the camp for its history and how it is so rough it is pretty.

I think it is important to note that the citizens of other Montana towns don't get this treatment.
Not many have heard of Havre and if asked the name of the capital their memories go stagnant.
It seems more people who know about the Big Sky can draw Butte to the front of their mind.
It is not because of Evel or his boy Robbie many know Butte for the copper that was mined.

Oh sure, I have taken the jabs about the hole in the ground and being from Gluteus Maximas.
Being from Butte it rolls off me like water on a duck or an insult to the Madam at the Dumas.
Butte has been beat up over the years and that is expected by those who don't understand.
I know differently, Butte is very special and at a time it was rip roaring and quite grand.

I had my share of bar fights because I was from Butte and my opponent needed to prove his metal.
In all honesty though being from Butte has more doors for me and this is the point I am trying to settle.
If you're from Butte you have a demeanor that precedes you as you walk through life's door.
You know no strangers, you're the humble salt of the earth and you are solid to the core.

As I reflect on my upbringing and being from Butte I know life could have been far worse.
I could have been born in New York City where being caring and friendly is considered a curse.
Being from the Mining City has kept me grounded for all that life has tossed my way.
And for those born elsewhere, I feel for you folks and for your souls I will continue to pray.

I made this far.

I took to morning whiskey as if I were a flea that jumps on a warm ankle.
Getting well was the nature of my beast, making life anything but tranquil.
As rare as a Panda's birth became the measure of you catching me sober.
Some say drinking was a choice I made, that observation falls short on the order.

I did not request for the drinking fuse to be lit with a fire generations old.
 A switch was thrown on and I stayed locked into the Irish drinking fold.
Broken glass and broken spirit became a slow changing kaleidoscope.
Bloody fingers twisting the damaged container in search of life hope.

Vision is bound to be distorted with focus seen in the bottom of a glass.
The fear of facing my damaged life made it easy for a drink to never pass.
It was nothing God like, nor touched by a spirit, no reform to inspire.
It simply came down to the primitive fact when living became a desire.

This morning the sun was calling me out with very little dread.
There was no Irish coffee needed to clear out drinking's cobweb.
I did not need to do a bump of coke or search for a remedy.
I am living a good life and that is in spite of the weaker me.

So I shall pat my blind dog on his head, thankful for his duty.
I reflect on the toll taken on many in the false claim of a party.
Like every other biped on earth I will have to face life's times.
Such how to close out all of my stories when it requires it rhymes.

Natures Regulator.

No matter your vocation or the amount money you have holed up in a bank.
There are great regulators at play in the universe no matter your title or rank.
Some are God's gentle hand correcting your course to keep vessel afloat.
But when it nothing but man's actions against nature she will turn remote.

The regulator I believe to be nature's assassin to able to bring the biggest of men down.
It has to be the encounter with the skunk whose burning odor nowhere else can be found.
If you are traveling on roads you might pass through a cloud left by a skunk now termed road kill.
The smell can penetrate walls and those who are in the line of fire learn to be alone and sit still.

Two grade school pals Donnie and Tim were leading the charge as we conquered Timber Butte.
How it got the name is a question for the scholars as I only saw knapweed and sagebrush take root.
It was not our first time scaling old baldy it was an easy daytime expedition we had mastered before.
It is what happened two hours into the conquest that went down in our neighborhood lore.

Tim had a homemade bow and arrow that he had been in R and D over the past two days.
He and his method of doom had been missing sparrows and crows leaving them without even a graze.
Donnie spied the skunk and Tim let the projectile fly hitting their prey which was soon dead in its tracks.
You know where it ends, the skunk pulled the trigger as his tormentors poke a stick to his back.

Thank God it was summer because they both slept outside that tomato juice seemed not to work.
Their mothers burned their clothes, that in itself was a big thing and both of them felt like a jerk.
It was a good thing Donnie and Tim got along because it was each other's company they had for a week.
And every rare time I come across that acrid stench I remember cute ones are just as capable to wreak.

My first taste of Whiskey. The Water of life

We were up at Uncle Joes and Aunt Helens in Walkerville for one of the Rodgers kids birthday party.
It was the usual fair, all the families were there and despite the foot of snow no one was tardy.
We had been dropped off by my Dad, he was working second shift at the old Butte Fire Station.
The party got under way, the women laughed and drank coffee and the men had the usual libation.

The party progressed the men went to the bar, oh Lord how I enjoyed the company of my cousins.
We all got along, looked out for each and other our electricity kept the family homes a buzzin'.
Cake and Ice Cream were about to get served when I had a tooth ache and ended the fun.
It was a miserable pain, so bad I had no cake and would have shot myself had I a gun.

The diagnosis was made, my mother acted quickly and a call was made to our dentist.
Doc Bartolletti confirmed the tooth had to come out, be at his office and he'd make room on his list.
Now logistics became a big problem, the snow storm had us all hostage up on the richest hill.
So my mother decided to walk my crying ass down Main Street and hopefully not take a spill.

I got bundled up tightly as did my Mom and then I think Aunt Helen came up with a plan.
Take a small bottle of whiskey, a few cotton balls and anesthesia would be done as down the hill we ran.
The provisions were gathered, and I was told whiskey would surely stop the all the terrible pain.
The cotton was soaked, additional whiskey Mom would tote and I would be in grand shape once again.

No surprise here but I truly enjoyed the straight whiskey and asked for more as we started to walk.
For the duration of the hike, my Mom kept the whiskey flowing and at my toothache I continued to balk.
By the time we hit the uptown I was swinging on snow clouds only wanting to visit and talk.
Sam told me as we plowed on in the storm to keep my mouth shut, suck on the cotton and continue to walk.

Seems whiskey made me quite social, I was quite happy with the prognosis of the numbed tooth.
Had I had a few bucks I would have stopped at the tavern and had a toddy with Sam in the corner booth.
We got to Doc Bartoletti's he made room on his schedule and sat me down to look at the trouble.
He asked me why I smelt of whiskey, I told him I had a shot or a maybe it was a double.

He went and asked my Mom what had happened and why my breath was that of a miner.
She told him she used the Irish sedation of the old and for children who are a known as a crier.
Doc walked into the office and gave me a wink and asked me if I was in pain.
I said no I feel quite good and would gladly do the snowy mile walk again.
The tooth came out without a hitch; Doc Bartolletti was an efficient worker.
Then with Sam as my guide and I staggered on home and that is my first taste of liquor.

N(one)un.

It is far from elite, it does come with a price and the toll tendered comes not all out of pocket.
All forced to wear pants named after seasonings, the shirts the color of skies on God's palette.
Committed to the word of the Lord, but only if it is the newer version, written after the fact.
The wardens of the institution rattle beads not keys, enforcing their laws on how all are to act.

When in a bar fight the unwritten rules state it is best to take out the opposing crew's giant.
The thinking is if the biggest threat falls to the ground, all others will be beaten and compliant.
In the education of their charges, all are clean targets for discipline and size does not matter.
There were no weight classes or categories instituted and no rules for skinny or those fatter.

Using knotted up fist, the ham bone of doom, the Black Veiled Monster strikes clean and fast.
With the Pope as the bouncer and millions of followers there has to be someone who's last.
Indoctrinated like Hitler's Youth movement, the children are pawns and the targets of wrath.
There was no court hearing or debating the crime, it was the Nuns violence awarded a path.

This one sided judgment drew its line in the sand when it came to how they punished a girl.
 I am sure they would have liked to take the gloves off with the fillies, willing to give it a whirl.
Old school sensibilities spared the girl rule violators from a smack with a taste of back hand.
When it came to boys, the women whose vaginas were dust, knew how to leave their brand.

It could be a swift swat to the head, a clip to the ear yet I have been witness to more severe.
I have seen knots that were egg like and a couple of bruises the rewards of showing no fear.
Never an appeal made to the parents who paid religiously for the boot camp that we attended.
Without hearing side two of the one track conversation, no matter the abuse rules are upended.

 You had it coming, you must have done something wrong was the justification of the attack.
 I have some news for the gnarly little thugs who liked to hit when one turns their back.
Your swift use of corporal punishment did me no good and actually had no effect at all.
I only wish I could be there to testify against you, when and if you see God's judgment hall.

Some will say that I'm bitter that I should forgive and forget and let old sleeping dogs rest.
To you I say enjoy your sanctimonious review of my life, I really have to contest and protest.
Look at the Magdalene Laundry and you will realize the punishment was not in God's name.
The little mean cowards who never knew the love of a man need to hang their head in shame.

Finlen

I woke up naked at the Finlen Hotel so it must have been a hell of a night.
The trouble is I had not made reservations here so try to imagine my fright.
I made a pillow out of my clothes so I will have to get dressed then sheepishly move on,
I am afraid to look at my cell phone photos, oh shit my wallet is gone.

Here's the first picture, I seem to be the OK, and I'm at the M&M drinking a beer.
The next one seems harmless enough, how did they fit all those people in here?
Oh now the plot thickens I vaguely remember that Butte girl with the red hair.
The next photo shows us doing some shots, we seem to be drinking with flair.

Oh oh here she is slapping me hard I remember putting my hand up a kilt.
Damn the kilt belonged to a Bag Piper, I obviously drank more than I spilt.
Ok the next one show's me raising hell, I am drinking at Maloney's bar.
They just might want to arrest me, the next one show me pissing on a cop's car.

Here is the next picture, oh Lord I'm ashamed, this is where my memory begins to fade.
Oh this one explains the cheek cut and black eye, I feel like I have been hit by a spade.
What in the hell was I thinking, in this one I'm standing pant less at Park and Main.
It has got to be 30 degrees and I am obviously feeling no pain.
Oh wait the next picture shows I am dressed again, my God that gives me relief.
Damn it the next picture shows their around my ankles again, oh how I feel the grief.

So how did I end up at the Helsinki, and who's the guy with the big dead grasshopper?
They called it yacht club, I don't see a boat just a hole where they used to mine copper.
I am back uptown in the next photo, I kind of remember this part.
Damn it my pants are down again, I'm outside the Terminal mart.
Well thankfully the photos stop here, for more details I will wrack my brain,
Oh God I hurt, I spent all my money but next year I will be back again.

Impromptu Sainthood at the altar of Saint Lawrence Church.

Cremation has become the way to leave earths bound among the older Irish these days.
Gone are the days of discordant three day wakes all while drinking the town a blaze.
A photograph does fine for those who visit the family at the Duggan Dolan Funeral parlor.
Both my folks went this way as did many other Irish the low cost appeals to the blue collar.

Once the funeral is over, the good byes are said the ashes are placed for internment.
Life seems to once again move forward, but to my Mothers ashes there is more sentiment.
My brother Mike had a small amount of my Moms ashes placed in small ornamental box.
A remembrance if you will for mom's sister Marg to keep instead of the traditional hair locks.

My Aunt Marg Cannon was a pistol, no truer Walkerville girl could you ever find.

My Aunt Helen the youngest sister of the three McDonalds was as equally fun and kind.
 Marg was a practical one and she deemed it would not be good for Sam to sit on a shelf.
There had to be a better place for the box so Marg took the matter of placement upon herself.

Marg lived on O'Neal Street, and the girls grew up in the shadow of the Church for Saint Lawrence.
So Marg gave it a thought and decided to keep my Mom on the right side of God's Fence.
On a Saturday morning she took a stroll to the church in her pocket my dear mother's ashes.
She entered the church, promptly blessed herself and headed for the altar in short dashes.

She got behind the main altar and with the help of the custodian they pulled back the grand altars top.
It was hallowed underneath and how Marg knew of this design fault is a mystery best left for a cop.
With a flick of her wrist she placed the box in its safe place nesting next to a few of the church relics.
She and her accomplice swore secrecy to each other as they sealed the altar back up in a matter of licks.

Marg then sat for a while in the first pew and recalled her great life that she had with her sisters.
She was confident in her actions, in her book Sam was a Saint, and protected from hells burning blisters.
To this day they remain there and I know this story is true because I heard it from my dear Aunt.
When she told me the story she had a great impish smile and with her actions she was content.

Now I am quite sure just as this story stands that the Vatican would frown on this tutelage.
I not sure how bad but I am thinking it would go over like Mother's Day at an Irish orphanage.
I take pleasure in knowing my Mom is being part of weddings and the baptism of all children she loved.
And whether the church participants know it or not, a saint of a woman watched them marry and be baptized above.

Illusion of McQueen.

Storied magicians have performed incredible acts of illusion, making the unimaginable disappear.
Copperfield's magic made the Statue of Liberty vanish, he did the same with a plane the next year.
It took him decades of practice and his study of other magicians for the deception to be pulled off,
Millions watched the magical illusion occur, stopping cold his critics that doubted and scoffed.

All trickery and deceit requires is that you distract your audience, the sure use of the sleight of hand.
They can make a nickel disappear and then magically reappear sealed with the "Ta Da" of the band.
Magical illusions of the entertainers packed ball rooms in Vegas and the Boardwalk on the Atlantic.
It's too late for my idea, but if it could have been accomplished, all Butte would be quite ecstatic.

The idea is simple and it would have taken great preparation, but I am sure it could have been done.
Cover all of McQeen and the other great communities with a large curtain hiding each and every one.
Each community would disappear for a brief moment and with the clap of the hands it comes back.
It would be an unbelievable grief if the trick took a bad turn and the trick planning fell off the track.

This illusion was never discussed on the sixth floor of The Company, they had another devious plan.
Like a dirty street fighter, the Company gave Mining City a few kicks and a smack with a back hand.
When you thought you had seen all the rotten tricks, The Company would pull another from their bag.
A swift kick to the shins and Butte forgot the moment; The Company land poachers filled another tag.

I imagine the production would have been immense and the disappearing acts the main show.
I heard once that Carson's Tonight show debated filming at Luigi's, so that is where I would go.
A flip of the curtain and the Sacred Heart Church and all McQueen would reappear in all its glory.
The act would be repeated again and again which would be a preferred ending for this story.

We know how this story ends, as they buried a piece of each community one building at a time.
In the final years as I visited these failing villages the conversation became hushed and sublime.
Generations who took community pride and built the church and homes with their own hands.
Lost was all, as the loaded dice used in this grift helped the Company, no matter how the dice land.

Oh, to bring them all back would be such a show, as the smaller pockets of history appeared.
All the teachings of Grand Parents would still be in place, all children being properly reared.
As with all magic acts they lose their appeal once the audience sees' how the trick is done.
Using a deck of marked cards, the Company stole the pot and Butte should have pulled a gun.

I know that my story may stir up some memories and not always do they end as we wish.
The Company money bought the law to rob Butte and steal the lives from this ethnic dish.
The communities were swallowed in record time and The Company then wanted dessert.
They got the Berkley Lake to wash it all down regardless of how many people they hurt.

The buildings and people may be gone, their images captured and left in a hall closet.
Not one of those souls, who came from these most unusual of places, is hurt or totally beset.
The Company could not bury the good souls and they left Butte worse than they found it.
If there were a show for destroying buildings in Butte, The Company would sell you the ticket.

See ya now.

If you are not from Butte the saying good bye to one another can be very confusing.
I've had friends with me after introducing themselves and the looks at good bye are confusing.
Instead of just "See ya" and then moving on Butte folks add the time frame of "now."
If you give it some thought they are correct in the puzzled look and quizzical furrowed brow.

Again it is the mystery of Butte that makes it a bit different from the rest of the state.
The phrase is not heard anywhere else I know of and that is what makes this so great.
Take a moment to ponder the phrase and I assume you will agree it is more of a greeting.
When you say "goodbye" or "talk to you later" it is appropriate when you are fleeing.

To say "see ya now" is the opposite of the goodbye of the phrase "I'll see you later".
I "see ya now" appears to be a phrase one would use when playing peekaboo with a little tater.
I "See ya know" should be answered with "of course you can dummy, I'm standing right here".
Only in Butte can a salutation be spun around to say goodbye after you enjoyed a beer.

I have heard the term "Youze Guys" but I have also heard that in New York and the Bronx.
I have rattled my head and researched "See ya Now" and it is only heard in Butte where it belongs.
But the good bye that is mixed with a present time frame that actually makes no grammar sense.
Unless you're from Butte, then it is second nature and all others are on the opposite fence.

My buddy Kurt Pentacost bartended at about every bar said the phrase with laughter and glee.
Kurt saw the irony of the phrase long ago but to the rest of us it is just part of our history.
Once again good old Butte stands out as an original but it never takes the time for a bow.
I got to get running, dinners waiting on the table, you guessed it, "I'll see ya now."

My Butte Moms

Before Hillary came to the table with it takes a village to raise a child it was the way of life in Butte.
Butte folk always had many Butte Moms who had all our safety and best interest deep in their root.
Down the alley and up the street was a Butte Mom who me and others she chose to christen.
I with you was one of their charges, my conscience when I went astray as they took the time to listen.

Their attention was not wasted on whether my shirt tail was tucked in or if my hair had a straight part.
It was if I was doing OK, how was my family the pleasant short inquisitions addressed from the heart.
You woke up on their couch and made you stay for coffee before you went on your way.
 Butte Moms were your family while growing up which how you feel about each other to this day.

Butte Moms are at your house after a funeral catering to your needs then they somehow disappear.
Butte Moms are front row at weddings always sure the one who drank too much avoided another beer.
They made the sign of the cross as you went out and were glad to see you making it home as they went to church.
Butte Moms raised us all and we came out OK and to look for any better would be a futile search.

I can only relive Mother's Day in my memories but that's not the note to end on.
I look at the women of my life in a much higher respect, the sign I hope of a good son.
No matter what I do I will always acknowledge all the great Butte Mom's in my life.
And when I find those find all those traits rolled together, I'll think about making that woman my wife.

Mesopust!

Another great thing about growing up in Butte was the depth of ethnic diversity.
It was like going to college and bunking with the Heinz 57 of ethnicity.
I saw Greek weddings where crowns were placed on the bride and groom's head.
And there is nothing better than the "I don't want her" polka when a Bohunk gets wed.

Butte has always held great public celebrations such as the Fourth of July parade.
There was a grand salute on Miners Union Day celebrating struggles for a fair pay grade.
Closer to home it meant some ones Grand Mother celebrated the holidays by baking Povatica.
There is also one East European celebration named Mesopust that was a big in Butte and Anaconda.

The Slavic community, the Bohunks of the McQeen Club and the East Side Athletic Club
Held the trial for the Mesopust the bringer of all bad luck and whose effigy they would drub.
It was the Bohunks way of putting the bad events of last year on the Mesopust whom they will burn.
Once the demon is dispatched great success follows all revelers for the New Year money they will earn.

For those of us visitors to the big party and not fully understanding it's social and mystical implication.
Soon realized it probably was not a good idea to find humor in hiding Mesopust before his annihilation.
This was exactly the plan Steve Osborne and Kenny LeCoure as they thought would liven this cold night.
They would not steal Mesopust but hide him but good before the burning took place at midnight.

The patrons of the East Side Athletic Club were a tight knit group and all for one attitude.
So when two outsiders were seen handling the Mesopust the East Siders considered these guests rude.
Ozzy and Kenny were quickly confronted and I can honestly say they took the threats serious.

Both returned to the bar, gathered their wits and as word spread in the club the Bohunks got furious.
Three was angry talk and finger pointing and the threats of serious harm for the Scoop Bar cad.
With a good read on the prevailing circumstances they decided to get going while the going could be had
They retreated to their truck and a few of us followed heading out before Mesapust burned.
Don't mess with a party put together by East Side Bohunks was the life lesson we all learned.

Maloney's The Vatican of Butte Bars

When a bar is sold the décor is redone and changes put in place that reflects the owner's taste.
Some change the name but at Maloney's Bar it is the pictures on the men's bathroom they did paste.
The bar stools are the same and the original named stayed for no real gimmicks are needed here.
Its own by two Irishmen who bought this crack in the wall and from the start their message was clear.

There is no fancy lighting, the back bar is the original as are the patrons who darken the door.
There are bar tabs that are needed to be paid at the end of the shift or you will drink there no more.
You would have to be stupid and brave at the same time if you think it is a good place to fight.
It may come off as a dive to those from the big cities but to Geno and Paddy M. it's no slight.

Maloney's bar is like an old friend that when you stop for a visit they haven't changed with the years.
You are welcomed with a greeting from who may be walking the plank that is honest and totally sincere.
It is the center of the universe on Saint Paddy's Day people make the pilgrimage as if it were Lourdes.
Good luck getting a seat in the place on the saint's day never the less try to get through the doors.

There is no cash machine, no ATM but if they know you well they might take a personal check.
It's a place where you can leave your drinking money on the bar with no worry or giving a heck.
I have seen more than a few folks who left said money on the bar and then went to go bar hopping.
The cash is scooped up, placed behind the bar with their name on it no chance of ever a robbing.

Maloney's is as true as a neighborhood pub though it is placed uptown in the historic Mining City.
It seems that there is no such person feels like a stranger but hold back on feeling happy and giddy.
Some out of town visitors make them self's at home it is easy to feel as if your part of the clan.
Just remember to behave yourself while you're drinking or on the Main Street curb you will land.

One of the best Saint Patrick's Day I can recall is when I got to pull beer duty in the bars cellar.
The beer was sent up to the bartenders through a trap door at the request of a bar tenders loud holler.
I and my brothers had some great times in the bar and it was not because we were treated as a king.
It is because of the owners and our good friends at this watering hole and it is for that its praises I sing.

Lou and Sam practice Urban renewal.

When you live on one street for all of your life and you know you are not going anywhere,
You not only look out for your house you also look out for your neighbor's kids and ware.
These diligences also include any property that is vacant and the happenings behind said walls.
It is looking out for yourself and taking up civic pride answering the bell when good citizen calls.

Our neighborhood was settled in the early 1900's and bustling businesses and commerce it had.
It was a well-kept neighborhood the majority of home owners took pride in their property they had.
So when a piece of real estate started to deteriorate quite quickly soon after the owner passed on.

Our neighbor Lou Martell who saw the building night and day made a wish the shack would be gone.
Once again because of the nature of this story and the antics on the part of all the participants,
My Mom and Lou did commit a felony of sorts and the Fire department was aware of the circumstance.
A recent ordinance had been passed about this time when Butte had a rash of suspicious fires,
It stated a structure had to be razed once it caught fire to stop it becoming unsightly mire.

Armed with this knowledge and fed up with neighborhood kids drinking beer and sneaking a smoke.
Lou and my Mom decided that a small fire would turn this impromptu club house into a forgotten joke.
It was a Saturday afternoon and the neighborhood was humming as the two headed up the alley.
They went into the building just far enough and set a small fire while they continued to be stealthy.

Happy with the small but very smoky fire they beat feet back to our house and placed the call.
"There was a house fire" was the report, and soon the dispatcher started rolling the proverbial ball.
Within a few minute the pumper truck arrived it was small so there was no need for the fire hydrant.
The inferno was stifled in a matter of minutes, my Mom and Lou told on themselves as malcontents.

They knew the fire crew by first name as my Father fought fires in Butte for over 25 years.
They confessed one the spot explained their plan for urban renewal and the danger they fear.
The fireman lightly shook his head but understood with a grin the incident was dismissed on the spot.
Soon the building was gone, Lou and Sam were happy and we had a place to play on the empty lot.

Kevin's Irish Cock.

Among the signs and photo's on the walls at Maloneys Bar is a picture of my late brother Kevin.
"Have fun on St. Patrick's day, but not as much as Kevin" is the caption. A fair warning to all times seven.
Kevin was a character to no end. If you met Kevin once in one hour he shook you hand fifty times.

It was hard drinking that took Kevin down; his glorious thirst and hard living were Kevin's only crimes.
How Kevin came up with one particular stunt to be used on the parade route of St. Paddy's Day.
Had me scratching my head all while shaking it too, and for a chicken I did have to pray.
Kevin grabbed a chicken, it might have been a small rooster, and decided to spray paint it green.
The plan was then to tie the poor green fowl around his waist under a trench coat sight unseen.

I witnessed the dress rehearsal for the stunt on Nevada Street in the back yard of Kevin's house.
He would yell,"Wanna see my Irish Cock?" The coat opened to show the spray painted green grouse.
The chicken was flapping and screaching as it hung upside down, Good God it was a horrendous sight.
Then he would laugh and headed uptown to the parade route roaring ahead with all his might.

I ran into Kevin the next day, and asked what happened to the green spray painted bird.
He had no idea, it finally made its break about ten o'clock and ran up Nevada to Third.
The poor creature must have been fine as Kevin explained that the fowl left on its own power.
I thought to myself "The poor fucking bird must be looking for an AA meeting and a hot shower."

It's not a pit, it's a lake.

There are many man made scars and blights against nature on the face of dear Mother Earth.
When topping mountains for coal in the East it's far away from prying eyes not near the family hearth.
There are toxic waste dumps in the North East who's only sign of existence is an occasional dead fish.
Most of the scourges against humanity are hidden and buried; they disappeared like a childhood wish.

They call them hog lagoons in the South where the toxic waste of commercial hog farms sit and ferment.
Surrounded by dams of clay I doubt it would be any better if they were contained in cement.
The lagoons of waste are hidden by acreage owned by corporations who do not care.
It's the price of doing business, look at the jobs it creates, trust us and do not despair.

There was Three Mile Island and Chernobyl. They are both sealed and out of sight.
The death, the loss, is all forgotten, they disappeared with the headlines overnight.
There are thousands of these sites around the world most are hidden from our vision.
And that brings me to Butte and the Berkley Pit, created by a corporate decision.

I call it the Berkley pit still to this day though geologically it qualifies as a lake.
It took over 60 years to get to this point and no one in Butte knew what was at stake.
I am quite sure that there a few corporate bastards who knew what would happen.
The pumps were turned off, the risk would rise and the corporate profits would fatten.

At first there were the water falls splashing off the north face and they looked quite stunning.
Water continues to flow because the corporation found it was unprofitable to keep the pumps running.
"What the hell" they said "we'll let the water flow, it's only Butte, can you please pass the butter."
As long as golf club memberships were paid, they thought they would leave Butte without a rudder.

It is now a Super Fund site for the EPA, and I do applaud the efforts and money well spent.
I am not a fool; I know that not all the profits from the pit paid for the Company's office rent.
The Uke drivers and the machine operators along with others who worked in the pit made a good living.
It was a group agreement; they would pull every mineral out of the hole until the pit quite giving.

There might have been and engineer or two who for saw the development of Berkley Lake.
I don't believe anyone could for see the dead geese and the environment being at stake.
And like Butte at night the pit's view from above seems to take a mystical, magical light.
But during the day the scarring is apparent and it is no longer who's wrong or right.

There are environmentalists who look at the Berkley and see nothing but devastation.
As long as one takes that side of the argument I agree with out qualms or a reservation.
In the eyes of the Government it is but a stain of a long and prosperous enterprise.
I am sure if my grandfather could see it Butte today it would bring tears to his eyes.

Yet not all is sad when it comes to the pit leave it to Butte to come up with the answer.
They built a viewing platform topped with a gift shop on top of this environmental danger.
Yes, Butte took it in stride; they did what they could and made the best with what is on hand.
I urge you to find another place outside of Butte that turned a profit on top of poisoned land.

There are two ways I can go here one is to turn my back and disown the town I am from.
I can call it an ugly mess, tell all I am relieved that I moved and pretend all is peaceful and calm.
I like many others who fare from the Mining City have decided to do what is right.
I admit I'm from the proudest place on earth and keep Butte Tough in my hearts light.

Kathy Maloney

Again we bring our hearts to half mast, a glass of memories topped with her laugh.
Time takes another joy in an Irish lass, who guided her charges with gentle staff.
More than an arms full by any man's measure her embraces fulfilled our days.
The engaged lives touched by dear Kathy will remain in the memories of a sweet haze.

Kathy understood far better than most on the art of dealing with unfair limitations.
She took these setbacks and turned them into reasons for her uplifting visitations.
Her peace that has been found is what we all strive for, in all our kin's shortening lives.
Her wit as I recall, came as easy to Kathy and was as warming as the sun in the skies.

Held in the highest respect and appreciated even more for her cheer and quick smile.
Times got harder for Kathy as it moved on, yet she took it all in classic grace and style.
The pitfalls she faced could have beaten down the best yet Kathy understood the price.
She used days for laughter and her nights full of prayer conversing with God and Christ.

Those who know Kathy find relief in the knowledge that she is in a far happier place.
I look back at her map in life and for all the travels and friendships, far too many to trace.
It will always be an empty chair at the table; many out of habit will turn to see if she's there.
She is, you just don't see her as we are used to, but for ever we will feel her love and care.

Lake Berkley

Ed lived up the street from my family and drove a Uke full time at the Berkley Lake.
Son of a bitch, that just doesn't seem right, let me give this a second take.
I remember so well playing in our neighborhood and at hearing the noon siren,
It warned of the mid-day dynamite blast at the Lake, nope, I got to keep trying.

Say what you will about the damage done, the Lake had decent paying jobs.
That kind of works but still not close, it doesn't make sense that a miner bobs.
Let's give this a shot, People travel from 'round the world to see the Berkley Lake.
Ok, this is getting better; it all comes down to perception for goodness sake.

The painted walls of Lake Berkley would be a challenge for Grandma Moses to capture.
I think I have it now it is a simple Butte recipe take a man-made disaster and add water.
I almost forgot the secret ingredient for this Butte recipe without it would flop.
Butte toughness in accepting the situation and like sweet cream it floats to the top.

Other parts of the nations have abandoned mine sites and turn their heads at the past,
Butte took the flooding not as a danger and christened the pit into a Lake to last.
Gone are the days of the hustle and bustle of the Pit but Butte tough never cry's.
Butte tough looks at the mining scars and envisions the crow's feet of nature's eyes.

Some other parts of the world look at a Lake that could dissolve a cow in a week.
As a curse, a blight, a sign from the heavens that God's favor was for all to seek.
Butte in turn looked at the acidic water knowing full well it was a danger to touch.
They rebranded the Helsinki into a yacht club not thinking it at all a bit too much.

Making a purse from a sow's ear is not an original process limited to the Mining City.
What makes it Butte tough is that it takes its lumps as many others would seek out pity.
There will never be yacht races or a fishing derby held at this Lake that is no longer a pit.
What is for sure is that only Butte could turn a disaster into a tourist destination to visit.

Inside the Head of the Lady of the Rockies.

I was the mid 1970's when Bob O'Bill had a prayer answered and he vowed to keep his word.
I decided to visit the construction site and Joe Roberts to visit with him to verify what I had heard.
I went to his place of business with the purpose of interviewing the man some thought mad.
I had gone in skeptical and full of myself and as I spoke with him it realized I was a cad.

I first heard of his plans to put a Statue of the Blessed Virgin on the top of the great mountain divide.
I held my comments to myself and must admit like others, we thought common sense had taken a ride.
The feat he had set for himself and the community of Butte was monumental as well as grand.
He would put a massive statute on a place that few have walked up and had the courage to stand.

I went to visit Joe at his equipment shop and yard that had been there after the starting of the pit.
I had a line of questions to be answered before our conversation began and we could sit.
Joe had another idea and he waved me to his office door and we quietly took a stroll.
It seems that his vision had begun taking a form and this is the story that needs to be told.

We rounded the corner and I have to admit I was quite surprised and taken completely aback.
There off Montana Street I saw what Joe had seen for years on a journey he never lost track.
It was the head of the monument sitting right where it belonged and no longer in his mind.
At over 15 feet tall and stunning as we crouched to get inside his vision of which I had been blind.

It was explained to me by this man of faith that he did not complete this task on a whim or dare.
His sincerity and commitment to the project was not for tourism but to honor an answered prayer.
My youthful indiscretion of being one to mock this gift I truly felt was forgiven at that moment.
The Lady shines at night and that is how I learned on another's faith one should never comment.

I walked away from that afternoon meeting impressed on how a man could give so much.
I learned a lesson about my cocky self and how a man's dream became a treasure to touch.
I carry this story to you not to promote the project or with hopes to increase those who visit.
I write it for I remember the day I found humility and realized it's the prayer and not who gives it.

It has changed, and again not.

There is a Butte Rat toiling away in a cubicle and watching the clock in a major city somewhere.
The years away from Butte may have hardened their heart to where it simply no longer cares.
The miles and the absence from attending a Butte event bring a frown and shaking of the head.
"I'm glad I have missed that one" is whispered to oneself as if they were speaking of the dead.

There are the number crunchers that can statistically support why they avoid going back.
It really has not changed, it is one of the poorest counties, and it will never get back on track.
Those last few points are the reason the prodigal should perhaps take another look at Butte.
In order to justify their absence from their place of birth they are missing the main attribute.

It is because of the hard times and the struggles were embraced that makes Butte feel so alive.
Larger cities and Shanty's have taken smaller economical hits and surrendered the spirit to survive.
Butte takes a shot to the mouth, grins and spits out blood coyly asking, "Is that all you got?"
Those deniers of the fact they came from the salt of the earth need a more convincing thought.

The wayward Butte Rat chooses not to remember the hard times forgetting they really do pass.
They don't shy away from the hard times they have now, they learned to be strong in the past.
Every time they reach out to give a pan handler a buck it was to help they learned in their youth.
Yet they look at the spot on the Montana map and deny to themselves the God honest truth.

Here is the twist regarding gainsay as they are not putting Butte down on a shit list.
Their negative thoughts travel no further from their mind and nestle in ignorant bliss.
In the confines of the Butte city limits these thoughts have no life and fall like lead from the sky.
It is the negative thoughts that pave the streets of Butte's resilience never allowing it to die.

I know I would be living in an ice cream castle if I ignored the negatives of the Mining Camp.
I acknowledge them; they are standing right there next to the lawless district lit by red lamps.
This is about the poor son of a bitch who have succeeded and made a name for them self.
No matter their accomplishments they will never rest until they take their heritage off the shelf.

I yell to them "Come on in, the water is fine." And all parties know it is colder than hell.
The returning to Butte can become Mecca for the lost one to once again see the Richest Hill.
I know firsthand that seeing the Mining City again after the years have gone is a bit of a shock.
Trust me when I tell you the pilgrimage is well worth it, once you feel your hard heart unlock.

Inspiration from Mulcahy's.

"Back then..... Bars were part of growing up & had nothing to do with drinking. They were a part of a social life long gone now." Mary Mulcahy Driscoll.

I heard the stories from my Aunt's on how difficult it was operating a bar in Butte as the century turned.
There was cleaning that happened in shifts and the building was heated by the coal they burned.
So much could be said about an Irish family and how they operated their fine establishment.
They were never ending hours and the family pulled every shift to earn their keep and rent.

I often think I might have been born in the wrong time when I listen to these fine tales.
I have bartended in Irish bars before and I am quite sure in that era I could pour ales.
From comparing the notes I have retrieved from my memories and the stories told.
It seems there is a tear in the fabric and in comparison today's bars seem a bit cold.

Oh yes we know all the bartenders by their first name and perhaps the number of their children.
The times I am referring to have the same cordiality that was extended to both women and men.
The bar life was not at all a bad thing, to be in the bar life today means you are in the cups.
To the days of my Grandfather the bar was a clone of the favor for Ireland's homey pubs.

I am in no way applying disparaging remarks to the way the taverns of Butte are run.
Mike McGrath and Gene Riordan would beat me to a pulp by the time their done.
There is no special group I belong to that separates me from today's drinking group.
It is the individual's, it is the time in history's place I reach back to and try to recoup.

It is when bars were a social club, a bank, a post office and at times the confessional.
That the neighborhood bars were the cornerstones of every Butte clan is not mystical.
There was many an Irishman who came to Butte from the Emerald Isle their place of birth.
There first stop upon arrival was the Saloon run by another Irishman on the richest hill on earth.

It was where introductions were made and many job interviews took place in the bar.
The finding of living accommodations and where to get a sound meal were all for par.
Considering many traveled thousands of miles to the Wild West and distant land.
The Irish and other immigrants helped each other get established giving a helping hand.

The best saloons did not depend on the cost of a drink to bring miners in their doors.
It was the clientele, the familiarity of language and the comfort found that established this core.
I would be a fool to state that drink had nothing to do with why an Irishman would show up.
I do know for fact that it was the keeping of a home fire in the hearts and whiskey in the cup.

I have read a many stories of the great famine and how it brought about the immigration.
Traveling by ship and train for thousands of miles I admire their spirit and determination.
In my traveling days when I would relocate like a good Irishman I would find a friendly bar.
I am confident in saying these saloons of today cannot hold a candle to an original Butte Irish Bar.

Lake Berkley

Ed lived up the street from my family and drove a Uke full time at the Berkley Lake.
Son of a bitch, that just doesn't seem right, let me give this a second take.
I remember so well playing in our neighborhood and at hearing the noon siren,
It warned of the mid-day dynamite blast at the Lake, nope, I got to keep trying.

Say what you will about the damage done, the Lake had decent paying jobs.
That kind of works but still not close, it doesn't make sense that a miner bobs.
Let's give this a shot, People travel from 'round the world to see the Berkley Lake.
Ok, this is getting better; it all comes down to perception for goodness sake.

The painted walls of Lake Berkley would be a challenge for Grandma Moses to capture.
I think I have it now it is a simple Butte recipe take a man-made disaster and add water.
I almost forgot the secret ingredient for this Butte recipe without it would flop.
Butte toughness in accepting the situation and like sweet cream it floats to the top.

Other parts of the nations have abandoned mine sites and turn their heads at the past,
Butte took the flooding not as a danger and christened the pit into a Lake to last.
Gone are the days of the hustle and bustle of the Pit but Butte tough never cry's.
Butte tough looks at the mining scars and envisions the crow's feet of nature's eyes.

Some other parts of the world look at a Lake that could dissolve a cow in a week.
As a curse, a blight, a sign from the heavens that God's favor was for all to seek.
Butte in turn looked at the acidic water knowing full well it was a danger to touch.
They rebranded the Helsinki into a yacht club not thinking it at all a bit too much.

Making a purse from a sow's ear is not an original process limited to the Mining City.
What makes it Butte tough is that it takes its lumps as many others would seek out pity.
There will never be yacht races or a fishing derby held at this Lake that is no longer a pit.
What is for sure is that only Butte could turn a disaster into a tourist destination to visit.

Butte Tough II

You arrived by train in Butte at the Front Street train depot just after the turn of the century.
You gather your bag head up Utah Street and stop in St. Joes and give a prayer for the safe journey.
You would get out of St. Joes take a left and at the end of the block was my families bar and hotel.
I often think about the Butte Irish that made that journey in order to leave behind what had to be hell.

I write of the Irish because that is what I know, I never mean to shortchange any other settlers.
You write what is given to you but that does not mean other nationalities have no story tellers.
Butte was the great experiment in a grander scale than the rest of the world could imagine.
In the time of the earth Butte grand days were gone in the puff of a steam locomotive engine.

If Butte was a boxer the odds would laced up against it but even the bookies admire the heart.
I always believe that Butte has another round in it, hears the bell and is ready to start.
Butte always seems to be a contender and it does at times find itself sitting on top.
I often wonder what union picketers on a Butte job site are saying as nonunion has to stop.

I am still confused how Obama and his posse ended up celebrating the fourth in the mining camp.
I am not all that surprised to see Butte in the news it goes back to when Joe Lewis was champ.
Being from Butte I keep an eye out for the old girl when she comes up in a national conversation.
It doesn't surprise me when I hear distractors of Butte, people are free to make a wrong observation.

I shall keep cheering when Butte gets a break like when the Robbins brothers brought work back home.
I read of my Irish family and how they arrived and settled with others who would no longer roam.
Butte had it before and I believe it will have it again there is still more than a breath in the Copper town.
I have a strong feeling Butte will bounce back, we all know it is impossible to keep Butte Tough down.

Butte Plastic and the company store.

I relish in the proposals by disenchanted states to form their own union and currency.
There is never the threat to change religion or Mother Tongue spoken by all fluently.
The change of currency goes far back in time as it is the binding of power and control.
It is the use of store credit and feeding large families in the Mining Camp I wish to extol.

Jesus is said to have fed a large gathering using a few fish and a couple loaves of bread.
That miracle would have been handy for large families during the times everyone did dread.
It was not just the very hard times that were punctuated by death or loss of good health.
Feeding families that numbered close to a dozen or less required independent wealth.

I look at a rerun of The Andy Griffith Show and am taken aback by the prices listed for food.
Beef at nineteen cents a pound and bread for a dime helped in feeding a large brood.
Even with these prices when you a feeding a large crew the purse strings get stretched.
It is the use of credit at the neighborhood stores that in my mind is forever etched.

My Mom and Dad and other families in Saint Joes traded at the Supreme Market.
A massive metal rotating file system held all the receipts each in their own pocket.
The Supreme was about the size of the snack isle at the marketing beast Wal-Mart.
It had what was needed for the staples of meals and a Butcher to put meat in the cart.

There was never a "Special" or an advertised sale and the signs were done by hand.
Joe and Mary ran a good shop and truly understood where their customers did stand.
They knew every customer and the family by name and always kept the kids in line.
If you tried to sneak candy in to the order Joe or Mary called home to see if it was fine.

The yellow receipt for the purchase went with you, the original in the grand cabinet.
Partial payments were allowed with no interest charged which they did not regret.
The stores were far more than the place to get groceries and all parties understood.
They symbiotic fair business thrived in hard times with all doing the best they could.

The currency for the bill every month came from the pay checks that were earned.
Interest payments were handled with the payment of trust that was shared and learned.
I remember when the Supreme Market closed and my Dad went up to settle the bill.
I wondered around and visited with Chuck the Butcher, Dad and Joe made time to kill.

I was not aware of the agreement that was held, I was not privy to the business plans.
I'm sure work was verified and then character vouched, sealed with the shaking of hands.
The business was shuttered and I believe razed after Butte Urban Renewal done by fire.
It was a more than business as we all lived with the Butte answer to the company store.

Butte Nick Names

Wikipedia describes a nick name as familiar or humorous but sometimes a pointed or cruel name.
It is given to a person or place it states as a way to shorten a moniker and at times to bring shame.
Growing up in Butte I knew many men by their nick names I knew not what name their mother's did use.
But Butte stands apart from all others in giving nick names in jest and other times to amuse.

The first one I remember was Tony "The Trader" Konanica he had a huge trading post uptown.
He was a nice fella but his store was quite filthy, on the Fourth of July he dressed as a clown.
I ran with Joey Faroni he and his dad went by the nick name Muzzy.
I tried to find out how the creators of the wop chop got the name but the details are fuzzy.

Of course there is Bubba Maloney and I'm reaching here but I think it because he was a big guy.
There is Evel Knievel who got his name from the police or that's the story they want you buy.
There is my friend Danny,"Pumachelli" Uggetti, his name is a twist on his Gramma's pasta dish.
You buy your whiskey today from Bill "Chunky" Thatcher, ironically he used to drink like a fish.

My dad told me a story about a Centerville butcher who was nick named "Dirty Shirt McNabb"
That's the odd thing about nick names, they will last all your life until like all you end up on the slab.
Paul "Chubs " Cote and Tom "Dewey" Harrington and Tom "Maggot" Pelletier are a few I know.
There is no story on how they got their nick names and as with life the mystery will grow.

My Moms nickname was Sam, and some called my Dad," Jack", others called him "Meg".
Sam got her nick name for a World War Two man's haircut called a "Sammy" but Meg I have not been able to peg.
There was "Big Eye" Petritz and his nephews "Rooster" and "Yonk", oh the Bohunks loved a good name.
Bohunks is another, it's up there with "Wop" and "Harp" categorizing a race with no shame.

I grew up with Larry "Wop" Giovanini went to high school with Brian "Moose" Holland.
The bigger, the taller the better your chances of a Butte nick name you would finally land.
Some were quite cruel and whispered to each other like Stevie the Shoe Shine guy.
He was called Stevie "Waterhead" for a medical condition yet shoe shines many did buy.

There are so many names I would like to explore Butte was like an Italian mob.
Lefty Olson, Oaks Oneil, Chooksi Kasoon and Tuta Perini are just a few on these waters that bob.
So many have nick names even the owners are not sure how their monikers came about.
It is one of the great mysteries of Butte and in some cases I hope I will never find out.

Cathedral Windows on Nevada Street.

When I look at what Hollywood tells us is the perfect neighborhood is which to raise our children.
I know that it likely reflects the memories or dreams of the writer sent to the TV screen from his pen.
Whether it be stick ball in the Bronx or Andy and Opie heading to the lake to catch a fish.
It all paints a picture of the joys of love and family that so many try to contain in a wish.

Raised in Butte there really was no neighborhood greater than the one each of us lived in.
Our worlds were so much smaller yet because of those confines it is where this tale begins.
These are days when riding a bus meant an exploration of a distant part of the Mining City.
Good times were found in a few city blocks where our world was a safe and sheltered entity.

We supported the Kool Aid stands that some enterprising kids would set up just down the street.
When a building caught fire and the Fire department arrived we would gather to feel the heat.
These are the day's that are hard to explain to anyone who did not live in these care free times.
We supported each other, sharing what we did not have, doing without was no social crime.

We sold Christmas wrapping as fund raisers the only competition was a friendly test between classes.
It was healthy and I believe the lesson taught was to work for common good with no monetary clashes.
It was in a description a form of neighborhood socialism, though independent each family stood.
Be assured that we looked out for our own, yet this own encompassed the entire neighborhood.

In grade school my Mom came up with a Christmas vision that would adorn McGinley Manor.
She decided to use the wooden framed storm windows as a pallet for her latest artistic endeavor.
All though our family home would own the glass fresco that would be erected every Christmas season.
It became a project the entire neighborhood became part of and not one person debated the reason.

My Mom used a pourable plastic resin in which chards of broken glass would be formed and suspended.
It would be a multicolored interpretation of the Nativity scene taken down when Christmas ended.
The outline for the masterpiece was etched out by Sister Carol who shared Mom's vision of the project.
The gathering of the needed broken glass for the mosaic became a neighborhood mission to protect.

There were multiple colors as in the stained glass windows that seemed to be in every Butte building.
It was the collecting of these colorful samples of glass that united the neighborhood all including.
The Magi star was created by scavenged windshield glass, the other colors came from kids donations.
The blue came from crush up Noxema jars and it is the harvesting of other colors made the creation.

The tough Indian kids who respected my Mom and other times chased me to kick my ass.
The natives would drop by with samples of a kaleidoscope completely made of broken glass.
One particular Indian a tough fella by the name of Terry Falcon and a sworn enemy of mine.
Terry made a great effort to bring glass to my Mom, her smile made the tough Indian shine.

More than a few of the red train signal lights in our neighborhood got broken out that year.
My Mom put out a call to cancel the need of red glass for further vandalism she did fear.
There were coffee cans of Mountain Dew greens and stained yellow glass left on the family porch.
I'm glad my Mom had no use for charcoaled wood or many a building would have felt a torch.

The windows were done in time for Christmas and when lit up it was a glorious sight.
She won first place from the Montana Standard for the stained glass that lit up at night.
My Mom did make the homage to the good Lord Jesus and the three wise men.
She was the first one to thank the kids who collected the glass and made it all happen.

I know those days of such a fun filled youth will never be seen in my remaining time on earth.
When neighbors got involved in helping others and the only pay off was laughter and mirth.
I am far from being a curmudgeon and think that today's life is OK and well worth living.
I am confident in saying that we would be far better off with Butte's ideal sharing and giving.

Catholic Beatings. Do you kiss your mother with that mouth?

Growing up Catholic in Butte, your chances of getting cuffed by a member of the clergy were actually quite good.
At times it could be the Nuns who were able to inflict the most pain. But the novices did damage when they could.
I had my first introduction when I entered first grade at St. Joes, Sister Anna Patricia got so upset with a lad.
Elliot cried, Sister Patricia went postal, a girl named Gail voided her bladder and then it turned bad.

I have been on the receiving end of shots from the Christian Brothers and was pummeled by a math Teacher at Central.
I saw fish hooks administered, chest punches delivered and of course it was fruitless unless witnessed by all.
I was taught to always look at what one person might have gone through before you ran into each other that day.
When it came to the Sister Patricia she not only stubbed her toe, she hit her head, lost money and must have ran over a dog that was stray.

I am not the Lone Ranger when it comes to these stories, I saw more than a few of my school mates get the same treatment in class.
One such incident comes to mind involving Steve Seymore and Monsignor Harrington that occurred one day after mass.
The Monsignor was a stoic man, his firm jaw set place underneath a canopied hat that came with his holy position.
He pushed and slapped poor Steve down St. Joe's metal stairs with his hat still in place and backed by Irish tradition.

It was no good to complain to my parents, their reply to me was "I must have had it coming"
As far as postponing the punishments there was no place to which I could escape by running.
Yet here I am today no worse for the smacks and the cuffing's that were professionally delivered.
Their predictions of my failures are partially true; perhaps more beatings should have been administered.

Catholic Priests and the Rolling Stones.

Have you ever given a second thought to how the Rolling Stones became.
I am not talking about how they met at first, I question their second name.
"The Greatest Band in the World" is a questionable established moniker.
It was given to them by Mick and ever since then it has been hallow fixture.

Kiss called itself "The Hottest Band in the World" and it stayed on nicely.
Jackson was the self-proclaimed "King of Pop" which became dicey.
Colonel Tom made far more money with "The King of Rock and Roll"
We found out how far a false king falls and how pills can take a toll.

Ali was the "Champ" and in a twist of direction he proved he was.
That is only one of all titles I debated that brought me to pause.
So when someone proclaims them self to be the only top dog.
I take a step back and start debating using sense and the history log.
So here is where I am going, I proclaim that I am a recovering Catholic.
It is a common phrase used by many since the scandals made us sick.

This beating the church has taken is not the out I was looking for.
I got tired of man being God's agent, is when I headed for the door.
I remember very clearly the absolute arrogance of many a priest.
They forgot they were as human as others and their humility ceased.
Now relax all you catlickers sharpening the cross for me to be impaled.

I am happy victims got the cash paid and the pedophiles are jailed.
I am actually looking at the church once again, a second thought I guess.
I can forgive them as I have forgiven myself, for my life's drunken mess.
This new Pope seems down to earth and like Obama he would sit for a beer.
 If I see on priest doing Jagger's rooster walk, it is me they will have to fear.

Charlie's New Deal .

When one is away from Butte for more than a few years it seems easy to see all the changes.
The older neighborhoods like where I grew up have many homes in deteriorating stages.
I have written about Buttes answer to pubs the great Mining City neighborhood bar,
So many are gone and more than a few empty lots are what is left of this sentimental scar.

There is one particular watering hole that became a neighborhood stall worth and much more.
True like any other bar its primary business was serving drinks and the occasional bottle to go.
I speak of Charlie Judds New Deal and already I remember how Charlie and his better half Ester,
helped out so many Butte folk all while never allowing an ill feeling of others to fester.

Two of my Aunts lived in the Silver Bow Homes directly across the street from Judds bar.
Aunts Helen and Dorthy McGinley thought the whole Judd family especially Ester were the best by far.
I knew one thing for positive and that was Charlie's was the place for Butte kids at Halloween.
It was packed with children receiving tons of candy and the drinkers sat and enjoyed the scene.

Charlie's stayed opened for decades and the Judd boy's each went on their own path,
Mike worked the last shifts walking the plank, the bars closing was a matter of math.
It is not an easy life running a bar and as recent some of Butte's bar business has fallen off.
The Judd family closed its doors in response to the economy and they all moved out of the loft.

It was a hell of a bar when it was rolling and many a good night I enjoyed in the joint.
When the Bulldogs were playing at the stadium at half time to the bar we would point.
Charlie's is a stand-alone reminder like the head frames and the Grand Old Finlen Hotel.
It's a time when a family like the Judds looked out for all kids, to keep us from going to hell.

"What happened to Grandpa's leg?" "Oh, he lost it."

Growing up in the Mining City we have all know of family or friends who have been harmed or maimed.
It could be the loss of a digit in a piece of machinery or perhaps a car wreck is the reason they blamed.
My Uncle Joe Rodgers last a piece of his hand and I understand an errant wood saw was the culprit.
You would never even notice unless you looked very hard as it never took a toll on his great spirit.

I never had the opportunity to meet my grandfathers they both passed away when I was young.
What I do know about these Irish Butte settlers is through the praises from my parents they sung.
To stay say these Butte originals accomplished great things in their lives would be an understatement.
They both built Butte businesses from the ground up which is why I hold for them great sentiment.

I have to be honest their lives were never brought up or discussed much even at a family gathering.
Today we only have black and white crinkled photo's to remember their lives and their early passing.
There is one thing that these two men had in common and it is odd now that I take time to reflect.
Both of my grandfathers had only one leg and as I revisit their lives it brings out further respect.

Now this is the odd part of the story and it relates to my inquisitive nature and to hear tales of yore.
I asked if there was a reason both men had a tough time when they went shopping at the shoe store.
I have asked my brothers if they knew why we came from two double tough one legged Irishmen.
They had no answers to solve this puzzle for me and my Mom and Dad had this response for the clan.

"He lost it" and that was the answer, there was no further explanation offered to my simple question.
I did not ask more as I could see on their faces common sense told me there was no more explanation.
 I have taken many hours out of my life as I reviewed my family histories and this dead end story.
I have yet to find the answers at this station in my life but I imagine the facts to be quite gory.

I understand that there is a great possibility that the lost limbs can be related to the cursed diabetes.
Both men enjoyed the drink and I understand they both smoked which could close out this series.
I would like to imagine as I did in my youth the loss was by a gunshot during a bar fight that was unfair.
Perhaps they lost their legs in a war or better yet they were hunting and it was eaten by a grizzly bear.

I will never know the true story at this point the outcome of their lives are taken to family grave.
The loss of the legs is a small part of my Butte family history which I work on each day to save.
What I find most outstanding about this bit of my history is both men recovered and had great success.
 And I had better behave or they would come back from the grave and use their one leg to kick my ass.

You're not Butte Irish, go lay down by your dish.

You weren't beaten by Nuns, forced to wear Salt and Pepper corduroy pants to school and I doubt you had whiskey for breakfast for months in a row. You're not Butte Irish, Go lay down by your Dish.
You don't know what the consumption is, you never kissed the Bishops ring, and you have first cousins named Buffy, Angelo and Trey. You're not Butte Irish, now go lay down by your dish.
You wear buttons that ask strangers to kiss you, you only go to bars with friends and you think an Irish Car Bomb is a drink not a tool of the troubled times in Belfast. You're not Butte Irish, Go lay down by your dish.
You go to Butte Montana for Saint Paddy's day on spring break not because you were born there. You never received service from Elsie at the M and M or Dirty Mouth Jean at the Stockman or Jean at the Dumas Rooms, You're not Butte Irish, Go lay down by your dish.
You have no appreciation of the glorious thirst and the havoc it causes. Your Mother never muttered she should have eaten you while your bones were soft, you don't appreciate good arson, You went to the doctor to get well not the bar. You're not Butte Irish, Go lay down by your dish.
You spent good money on a green wig instead of buying another round; you think the Christian Brothers of Ireland is a brandy and you never shook hands with Babe or Bubba Maloney, You're not Butte Irish, go lay down by your dish.

You get pissed when someone wears orange on Saint Patrick's day, You love Notre Dame but you don't know why, Your Mom means more to you than your Dad, Your ears and nose keep growing till the day you die and you understand why I am writing this, Your Butte Irish, now go lay down by your dish.

Made in the USA
San Bernardino, CA
21 December 2015